WAITING FOR THE TIDE

A Radio Officer's memories of thirty years with the Hull Fishing Fleet...

ROBERT BAILLIE

RIVERHEAD

Robert Baillie

First published in Great Britain in 2017 by Riverhead

Disclaimer
Waiting For The Tide by Robert Baillie was published
posthumously in 2017. It was compiled from a collection of hand-
written notes, diaries and photographs left by the author.
Whilst every effort has been made to ensure that the information
in this book was correct at the time of publishing, the publisher
does not assume and hereby disclaims any liability to any party
for any loss, damage, or disruption caused by any errors or
omissions, whether such errors or omissions result from
negligence, accident or any other cause.

A CIP catalogue record for this book is
available from the British Library
ISBN 978-0-9929225-8-0

Design and Production by Riverhead
Kardomah 94,
94 Alfred Gelder Street, Hull HU1 2AN
Telephone: 07890 170063
email: mike.riverheadbooks@gmail.com
Printed by: Fisk Printers, Hull

WAITING FOR THE TIDE

Robert Baillie

This book is dedicated to my great grandson, Liam, the Laird, who gave me the inspiration to write it. He now has many yarns to read.
It has taken me two years to write it. I hope that everyone who reads it will appreciate how tough it was getting your cod to the table.

CHAPTER 1
A JEDBURGH BOY

I was born on September 8 1924 in the small Scottish town of Jedburgh, the eldest of eight children. My father was a clerk on the railway and my mother was from the hard working days of domestic service to the gentry.

Our first house was a tiny cottage in the shadows of Jedburgh Castle. The cottage had only two rooms and no running water inside. The toilet was outside and the only lighting was by oil lamps. But with a small orchard and a pretty garden, it was home.

At five, I started school, Jedburgh Grammar, which was a mile to walk from cottage to school. My interests were always outdoor activities. As I grew older I became a member of the cubs, then the scouts, where I had my first taste of leadership as patrol leader and engaged in my greatest love, outdoor camping and later on Rugby Union, when I joined Jedburgh Boys Club as a member of their team.

At fourteen, I left school and worked in a baker's shop. At fifteen war was declared and I joined Air Raid Precaution as a Junior Messenger. At sixteen years old I was called for an interview for a job at the laboratory with North British Rayon Co in Jedburgh. They made artificial silk used for parachutes and other articles. After a three-hour interview and an exam I was given the job as Assistant Analytical Chemist in the laboratory. This job was shift work including night shifts.

During this period I joined the newly formed Air Training Corps in Jedburgh and later attained the rank of Corporal. One of the earliest and most memorable things that happened to me was while I was on a day trip

Robert Baillie

to the R.A.F. aerodrome in Mac Merry, Edinburgh. I was picked for a flight in a Blenheim bomber flying to York. Not only was this my first flight but it was also my first time in England. The Air Training Corps was to prove invaluable to me in later life.

In 1942, after considering that I wanted to fly but also go to sea, I volunteered to join the aircrew in the Fleet-Air-Arm. I received papers to go to Edinburgh for a medical and to see the selection board. Here I was accepted to train as a Telegraphist-Air Gunner. Later my papers arrived and I was told to report to HMS Royal Arthur, Skegness, at the former Butlin's Camp that had been taken over by the Navy. From there we moved to HMS Vincent in Gosport to commence our aircrew training and from there to a drafting station in Dunfermline and then to Gourock in Glasgow.

We were next ferried off in the early hours of the morning to embark on the world's largest liner, The Queen Mary, and we set sail for New York. From there we went to Asberry Park, New Jersey, then to Montreal in Canada and eventually in 1944 to Yarmouth, Nova Scotia.

Here we trained for one year flying in a Swordfish open cockpit aircraft, firing open air guns.

At the end of the year we received our wings before moving to Lewiston in Maine to train in a Grumman Avenger, an American torpedo bomber.

During our time there two mates and I decided to use our twelve-day leave to hitchhike along the American eastern board coast via Portland, Boston and Rhode Island to New York. We did it spending the entire twelve days in New Jersey and New York.

During the time I was in America, my father was promoted to Stationmaster in Fife, so all the family moved from Jedburgh to this new abode.

After training in America we once again

embarked on The Queen Mary back to Britain.

Here, we trained at Inskip near Preston, night flying, then in Londonderry, Ireland where part of the training was with British Submarine. During our time there we were taken on board a submarine and out to sea where we had the great experience of diving and submerging in this vessel that give us an insight into what U-boat crews went through.

After completing this training my next destination was the Naval Base at Scapa Flow in the Orkneys where most of the home fleet was based. The train journey took me to Thurso, then I proceeded by ferry to Lyness Pier, Scapa, where I boarded the 'Dunlenis Castle' a depot ship for the movement of seamen. A small drifter came alongside and I was taken to the aircraft carrier HMS Trumpeter to be reunited with my pilot, Lt. Bunyon and observer, Sgt Alderson.

In the early hours of the morning we weighed anchor bound for my first engagement with the Germans, minelaying in the Norwegian Fiords. And from then on, it was minelaying and bombing the German shipping for the foreseeable future.

In the March we were ordered to escort a convoy that was taking arms and munitions to Murmansk in Russia. This was measurably the worst part of the war engagement where we encountered heavy pack ice and temperatures of -30° as we escorted the merchant ships through the Arctic seas. Although we got this convoy safely through we did lose two of our escort sloops to U-boat action.

While in Kola inlet on this convoy waiting for a return one to Britain I was transferred to the aircraft carrier HMS Campania to sit my exams to be promoted up to Officer-Air Gunner. On the return journey I was informed of my promotion.

The last raid we did was on a U-boat depot ship,

H.M.S. Trumpeter - Shipping strike, Norway - 4.5.1945

H.M.S. Trumpeter

H.M.S. Trumpeter - Convoy to Russia, 17.3.1945

H.M.S. Trumpeter - Convoy to Russia, 17.3.1945

H.M.S. Trumpeter

sinking it and probably two U-boats alongside it, near Harstad in Norway.

In May 1945 HMS Trumpeter and the naval force proceeded up the Skagerrak towards Copenhagen. As we steamed towards the Danish capital, the news came through that the war had ended. The German High Command had surrendered to our naval force, thus the war and the occupation of Norway and Denmark was brought to an end. Over the tannoy on HMS Trumpeter came the order 'splice the mainbrace'. Two large tots of rum for each of the crew followed.

From HMS Trumpeter, during August to October 1945, I was drafted to Crail Fife Air Station and then to Machrihanish Air Station on the Mull of Kintyre, where our squadron was disbanded.

Robert Baillie

Signature of holder. *R Baillie*
Date of Birth *8 - 9 - 1924*
Place of Birth *Jedburgh*

DESCRIPTION OF HOLDER.

Age *21* years.
Height *5* feet *6* inches.
Colour of Eyes *Brown*
Colour of Hair *Brown*
Complexion *Pale*
Any special peculiarities

This was the end of 846 Squadron, which I had the greatest pleasure to have served in.

From here I went to a flying control room on an aerodrome at Halesworth in Suffolk, then to a college near Salisbury to study business, from where I was demobbed in February 1946.

My passion was still with the sea so I enrolled at the Caledonian College in Edinburgh to take the Radio Officer's Certificate as I hoped to become a Radio Officer in the Merchant Navy. I successfully passed the certificate in August 1946 and proceeded to Marconi's in Leith, Edinburgh to join the Merchant Navy. Here I was informed that I was urgently required as a Radio Officer for the Hull Deep-Sea Fishing Fleet and that the money to be earned was high.

Marconi gave me an address: Kingston Steam Trawling Co., St Andrews Dock, Hull.

I wrote to them on Wednesday, October 9 1947 and received a telegram back from them the following day. It requested me to report to Hull on October 11 as I was to sail on the Kingston Chrysoberyl at 02.00 on Saturday, October 12.

This was the beginning of my 30 years sailing with the Hull fishing fleet, taking me to waters and destinations that I had encountered during my Russian convoy days on board HMS Trumpeter...

Robert Baillie

My 'first' ship, Kingston Chrysoberyl

CHAPTER 2
MY FIRST SHIP

On October 11 1947 at 18.00 hours, I arrived in Hull to join my 'first ship' the Kingston Chrysoberyl at St Andrews Dock. As I came out of Paragon Station I noticed the terrible devastation that the German bombers had inflicted on the city during the war.

Seeking directions to St Andrews Dock, I made my way down Hessle Road, before stopping an old fisherman named Billy Firth. He showed me the road to the tunnel and to St Andrews Dock and even to where Kingston Chrysoberyl would be berthed.

It was now dark but picking my way along the many trawlers moored there I found my ship all in darkness. I boarded the vessel and made my way aft, entered a small doorway and looked down a ladder where a small light was showing.

'Ahoy!' I shouted and a muffled voice replied, 'Who's that?'

'The Radio Operator,' I answered. A moment later an old gentleman appeared.

'I'm the watchman,' he said. 'Did you say Radio Operator?'

'That's right,' I confirmed and went down below and into the messroom. There was an oiled-fired lamp hung from the centre of the deck head. Peering round I noticed a large table surrounded by four bunks with closing doors, two very small cabins and a coal-fired stove.

The old watchman informed me that these were the quarters for the mate, Chief Engineer, Bosun, 2nd Engineer and Radio Operator. The retired ex-fisherman, now watchman gave me the full info on the ship. It was a steam trawler, coal-fired – had no baths or showers

The bustling St. Andrews Dock in 1956

and the only fresh water available you had to get out of a pump. The toilets, which were all made of iron, were across the open after-deck, situated on the port side aft, with seawater, pull a lever, look at the ocean, and wash away.

During my wait, engineers, firemen and deckhands were arriving. The first deckhand to come on board was a lad dressed in an ex-Navy greatcoat. He looked as if he'd just been demobbed. I introduced myself and he did the same. 'I'm George White, ex-Navy,' he said.

Next, a gentleman with a cap and pipe came over to me. He explained that he was Kingston's ship-runner George Watkinson and he asked me if I would sign on the log as I had arrived late.

'Have you any gear, bedding or anything with you?' he asked.

I replied that I didn't have anything apart from a sleeping bag. George nipped off for a couple of minutes and returned with a straw mattress and a pillow.

Meanwhile the dynamo had started and as the steam was raised the lights came on, so I was able to make my way to the bridge. One large steering wheel, one magnetic compass, one small, steam driven wheel all connected by chains to the rudder. Post aft in the corner was an old type echo sounder, where the bottom echo indicating was flashed on a horizontal dial as you pulled a switch.

I entered my radio-room on the starboard side of the bridge. It was no bigger than a small cupboard with one wooden seat, one transmitter, one receiver and one fixed loop direction finder - a single loop which you revolved and read off your bearing from a signal transmitted from shore. The final thing that I noticed was a large iron box with a cover and inside it were batteries, the type that had to be charged up.

Robert Baillie

To get from the bridge to the messroom and our quarters we had to dash in the open, regardless of the weather, over the deck and down through an opening via an iron ladder and you were there.

Another thing that surprised me was when I learned of our destination. I thought they fished the North Sea but I was wrong. This boat would soon be bound for the Russian coast...

Next I made my way to the bridge to meet the skipper. The original skipper, Sam Trolle, wasn't taking the ship for this voyage and in his place was Reuben Davey. On the bridge I met him, shook hands and then went off to my so-called radio-room. I sat down on the small wooden seat, took stock of my apparatus and switched on the receiver, transmitter and direction finder. I checked the state of the batteries and waited for the 'let go' signal from the bridge.

Slowly we eased away from the dockside and proceeded to the dock entrance, as it was tide time. The gates were open and out into the Humber we went, up the river, buoy by buoy to the Spurn Light Vessel and then onto Flamborough Head. Here was my first chance to test my direction finder. I tuned into the Flamborough call sign (FB) and as I could see it, checked out my D/F. Everything was okay. From here we steamed NNE through the North Sea to pick up Svino LH on the Norwegian coast.

Reuben Davey informed me that we would be going to the White Sea and through the Norwegian fiords. This entailed picking up a Norwegian Pilot at Lodingen and proceeding through the fiords to Honningsvag. To do this we had to give the pilots at Lodingen notice of our arrival, so here was my first action with my transmitter. I called Roervik Radio LGD and passed the message to Lodingen with our ETA. This was transmitted using Morse Code at about twenty words a minute. Roervik replied, 'Message received'.

The weather had now changed and a NE wind had sprung up to Force 8. We steadily sailed on to the West Fiord and entered the waters off Lodingen. The skipper then blew the ship's siren with the international signal 'G' for pilots and a few moments later a small cutter appeared from the shore with a pilot aboard. He climbed on board the Chrysoberyl and we were soon on our way again.

We hadn't gone far however when the chief engineer informed the skipper that we were short of water and a steam pipe had cracked and needed repairing. We docked at Harstad in the late afternoon and were informed that we would be there all night.

George White, the first deckhand that I had met when I joined the Kingston Chrysoberyl decided to go ashore and asked if I would like to go for a look around Harstad with him. We went into a small café for a beer but before we could have a beer we had to have a meal, or at least something to eat such as a cake or a bun, that was the rule.

George told me that his father, who was also called George, had been the Chief Engineer on the Loch Ard, which in late 1934 had sailed out of Hull and was never heard of again. The tragedy left his mother on her own and with six children to bring up. His mother ended up working hard to keep them all and was employed in Rank's flour mill and also braided fishing nets for the Kingston Steam Trawling Co.

Losing their menfolk was always a fear for women whose husbands, fathers and sons engaged in this most dangerous of jobs and would sail and never return.

During the time we were in Harstad another Hull trawler returning from the White Sea came in for fresh water. The skipper of this vessel informed our skipper that he was bound for Hull and was full up with plaice that they had caught at Cape Cherni, well out to the east. He brought his chart on board and showed us the exact position where he had caught the fish. Now I was informed that plaice brought a high price at market - above cod and haddock - and as our earnings were based on X amount of pounds to every £1,000 earned at market, this seemed to be the position to go for. We left Harstad and proceeded through the fiords passed Tromso and Hammerfest, then on to Honningsvag.

As we steamed along through the most picturesque scenery, I also had time to see more of this coal-fired ship. Looking down the grating into the stoke hold, I could see the firemen, endlessly shovelling tons of coal into the furnaces, and then the ashes being raked out and hauled up onto deck and dumped overboard.

Engineers were continuously going round oiling the engine, keeping the dynamo that delivered 110 volts D.C. for the lighting and the power for the radio's transmitter and battery charging. The standby navigation lights were paraffin lamps and their wicks had to be trimmed regularly to ensure their reliable operation.

I also saw the cook, working hard in his small galley. He baked bread and rolls every day to help feed over twenty crewmen.

There was no running water, it all had to be pumped up by hand.

All our beef was put into the fishroom where it was stowed in the ice used for icing the fish that was caught. But as some of the fishrooms were full of coal which had to be transferred to the stoke hold before fishing operations started, a lot of the meat was moved into casks full of brine, where it was salted, 'salt junk'. The casks were stowed on the upper deck aft.

The crew's quarters were for'ard under the foc'sle

and to get their meals meant another dash over the deck, again regardless of the weather.

The crew were fully occupied steaming off and getting the nets and fishrooms ready. The hours worked during fishing were eighteen hours on deck and six hours below.

We eventually arrived in Honningsvag and a cutter came off to pick up the pilot. It was getting dark as we left for our next day's steaming bound for Cape Cherni and the plaice fishing. The cutter with the pilot had just left when a dark object was sighted on our port bow. On examination, using binoculars the shout went up, 'It's a German floating mine!'

If it had continued on its present course it would have landed on the quayside in Honningsvag.

As we had no radio contact with anyone ashore we blew our siren to attract attention, hoping the cutter may hear us. He did, and came back out to us and we informed him of the mine. He dashed ashore to alert everyone. Later, we were informed that a Norwegian naval vessel had got the mine and it had been safely disarmed. Goodness knows what may have happened if the mine had hit the quay. It was amazingly lucky that we spotted it.

We sailed on, down Porsangerfiord, then along the Norwegian coast, passing Nord Kynn and along to Vardo. From there we left the Norwegian waters and entered Russian waters Tsipnavalock, passed Kildin Bank, Terebyska and along to the Sem Islands - all waters that I had ploughed through during Russian convoys to Murmansk - then eastwards to Cape Cherni and Svytanois.

When we arrived at Cape Cherni we sighted a few Hull trawlers and prepared to shoot our net and fish for this 'expensive new fish' called plaice. The weather was quite good but with moderate easterly winds of about

Robert Baillie

force 5 giving a cold temperature. It seemed that these were the best conditions for plaice fishing. The crew were all preparing the trawl gear ready for shooting and on the bridge the skipper was busy consulting charts and reckoning our position.

During my period in the Fleet Air-Arm I had experience of position finding and chart work as well as basic navigation. I found that on these vessels most of the positioning was dead reckoning and was also helped by how experienced you were following the fishing banks. I found that my experience during the war was going to prove a great benefit to the skipper in the future. This was especially true regarding position finding by radio and also with the more sophisticated position finders such as Loran 'A', which was used mainly by aircraft but later by the maritime services.

The crew were ready on deck and the skipper was in position. The trawl gear consisted of large bobbins and a fishing net connected by steel warps to a winch drum. The type of gear used depended on the condition of the sea bottom. Here the bottom was quite smooth.

The order was given to lower the nets and bobbins into the sea. The ship gradually manoeuvred to pay this gear away until it reached the bottom. From there the net would be towed for a certain time and then hauled back.

Meanwhile on the bridge, I discussed with the skipper that I would take radio direction bearings of Cape Kain, Svytanois and the Sem Islands. This would give a three-point bearing and would give us an idea of where we where. This was agreed on and resulted in my first encounter of putting a position on a fishing chart by radio. After a specified time the hauling process took place. The gear and net was slowly hauled up. This procedure was always on the starboard side. I watched as the warps came in, the doors came up and the bobbins were brought inboard. Then, there was the net, which the crew hauled on board with net hooks. Also now visible was what they called the cod-ends, where the fish were. This was slowly brought along for'ard and hauled on board.

I stood alongside Reuben Davey and watched the procedure. In the net was approximately 80 baskets of plaice. After releasing them on deck, the gear was payed away again for another haul. Meanwhile on deck the crew went into what they called fish pounds, where they proceeded to gut the plaice, throw them on the port side where they were washed, 'basketed down' and then sent to the fishroom to be iced and stowed ready for market. As I had a bit of time on my hands, I decided to borrow an oilskin frock, a pair of rubber boots and some rubber-gloves and join the crew gutting the plaice. When I arrived at the fish pounds the crew looked at me in amazement! A radio officer, on deck with the crew, gutting fish? But they were glad of the extra help. You have to remember that these men were working 18 hours on deck with just six hours below, which included their meal times.

Later in my career I would observe the terrible conditions these men endured, working on open decks with high winds, treacherous seas and temperatures as low as $-30°F$, among icebergs and pack ice and in the most inhospitable conditions that anyone could imagine. This was a job for the toughest men. Men who in the future I was going to be proud to sail with…

One of the busiest places on board ship was the fish storage rooms. When we left Hull we had at least two fish rooms full of coal. This coal was shovelled along to the coal-bunkers and the fish rooms were washed out. Down in the fish room members of the crew were engaged in storing the fish. This meant the

Robert Baillie

building of fish pounds with boards slotted in stanchions, and then the chopping of the ice. This was accomplished with axes, hacking away pounds of ice. When the washed fish was 'basketed down' it was stowed on shelves, which had been covered with the broken-up ice. Then, when enough fish was on the shelves, the ice was shovelled on top of it.

Day after day this went on. Shooting nets, towing and hauling nets, processing fish, until one had enough on board to go home.

On the bridge I used our only echo sounder for measuring the sea depths. This machine transmitted a continuous series of echoes to the bottom, which were reflected back to a receiver. And since the speed of sound through water is known, the depths could be calculated and recorded on a dial. If this machine failed, it was back to the lead and line.

I informed the skipper that I was fully acquainted with steering a ship and knew all about using the compass. From then on I was able to relieve him by doing spells of steerage and at the same time doing my radio work. The most important parts of this were receiving weather forecasts, which gave advance warnings of storms, the taking of D/F bearings and listening for messages from the shore coast stations.

The final member of the crew of a fishing vessel was undoubtedly one of the most important men on board – the cook.

When we left Hull we didn't have much in the way of bacon and eggs etc. on board, just enough for the first few days that was all. They relied on catching fish for food, so for the biggest part of the voyage it was fish for breakfast, fish for dinner, fish for tea and cold fish for supper. The cook though was a baker as well, fresh bread and rolls being baked for the crew daily. Then on the upper deck was our supply of salt junk meat. So potatoes, salt-junk and fish was our staple diet.

The day soon arrived when we had caught our compliment of fish and we were preparing to stow up and make for home. To give the skipper a chance of getting some sleep, I took the first spell on the wheel.

Our course home would be the reverse of our outward one, taking us passed Sem Island, Cape Teriberka, and Tsipnavalock on the Russian coast to Vardo, then along the Norwegian Coast to Nord Kyn and up the Porsangen Fiord to Honningsvag. Here we picked up a pilot and proceeded through the fiords to Lodingen, up West Fiord and then southerly down the Norwegian coast to Svino. From there we sailed through the North Sea to Flamborough, then to Spurn and up the Humber, anchoring off the clock tower. Then we waited for the tide and what number we had been given for the market sale.

While we were anchored my friend George White asked me where I was staying while we were in Hull. I informed him as I did not know Hull, I may go home to Scotland whilst we were in dock. It was then that George invited me to go to his mother's house for tea whilst I sorted out what I was going to do and he gave me his address.

When we docked I had to wait for radiomen to come on board in case I had any repairs to do. From there I proceeded to Hessle Road and after I got directions to George's mother's in Victoria Avenue, Wellstead Street, I arrived at her door and knocked.

When she opened the door I introduced myself as Bob, the radio operator from the Kingston Chrysoberyl. Fortunately George had alerted her of my arrival and she was expecting me.

Clara White, George's mother was typical of the tough women in the fishing fraternity.

Clara's husband George White, had been the

The trawler that vanished

HULL'S fishing community learned to live with tragedy.

Even so, losses were hard to bear at the best of times. But when husbands, fathers or sons vanished without trace the agony was intensified. . .

THE Loch Ard left St. Andrew's Dock on January 14, 1934, bound for the fishing grounds off Iceland.

Two days later she called at Aberdeen.

That was the last time that anybody saw her.

At first relatives were not too concerned, particularly as Loch Ard carried no radio.

Although the return trip to Iceland normally took only 23 or 24 days, it was not unusual for trawlers to "lay up" for days on end to ride out bad weather or, indeed, to become trapped in the ice.

Severe

But the weather around Iceland had been severe, even by its own atrocious standards, and as the days of waiting became weeks so the fishing community of Hull braced itself for the worst.

THE CREW

Skipper of the Loch Ard was BILL SHEARS, a 34-year old married man with two young children. The family lived at 24, Liverpool Street.

He came from an old Brixham seafaring family and had been sailing out of Hull for 12 years with various firms including Ross, Newington and Jutland. It was said that few skippers knew the Icelandic fishing grounds better than he.

Mate: W. R. FREER, aged 26, of 11, Filey Grove, Liverpool Street. Married with one child.

Bos'n: G. McHague, aged 24, of Palm Grove, Eastbourne Street. Married with one child.

Third hand: HENRY TURNER, aged 37, of 127, Gillett Street. Married with seven children.

Deck hand: T. WILSON, aged 33, of 5, Perseverance Terrace, St. Luke's Street. Married with two children.

Cook: JOHN BRADSHAW, aged 46, of 82, Manchester Street. Married with three children.

Spare hand: T. SHEPHERDSON, aged 20, of 11, Albert Terrace, Gillett Street, single, lived with mother.

Spare hand: GEORGE HOWE, aged 35, of 7, Gladstone Terrace, Courtney Street. Single, lived with parents.

Spare hand: J. MOONEY, aged 20, of 5, Harold's Terrace, Scarborough Street. Single, lived with mother.

Chief engineer: G. A. WHITE, aged 40, of 3, Wright Terrace, Manchester Street. Married with six children all under 14, one born two weeks ago.

Fireman: G. BLAND, aged 39, of 59, Sledmere Grove, North Road. Single, lived with niece.

Fireman: DANIEL LYNCH, aged 20, of 1, Albert Dock Terrace, Bean Street.

It was on Friday, March 2, that the Loch Ard was finally given up as lost and after six weeks of anxious waiting the crew's families were plunged into grief which was shared by the whole of the city.

The fate of the Loch Ard was never to be known for certain. But it seemed reasonable to assume that she was overwhelmed by the exceptionally heavy seas.

Widows

The Hull Daily Mail reported that the Hull port missionary, the Rev J. Summers, who had the unenviable task of breaking bad tidings to so many families in the 1930s, had the sad duty of informing seven Hull women that they were now widows. Twenty-two children were left fatherless.

"South-West Hull was a place of mourning and despair. Many blinds were drawn and women with little children tugging at their skirts in many a homestead were trying to hide their tears and sorrow," it reported.

Hull's bleak midwinter

■ THE James Long disappeared without trace in February, 1933 — the final act of tragedy for Hull that had seen the loss of the Endon, Cape Delgado, and Lord Deramore.

The Hellyers Bros. boat had steamed out of the Humber on January 29 bound for the Icelandic fishing grounds and was due back in the final week of February.

She was last seen homeward bound, but, although fitted with wireless, was never sighted or heard from again and on March 14 was officially posted as lost.

The James Long carried a crew of 13. All of them were married men and the disaster orphaned more Hull children than any which had occurred previously.

WAITING FOR THE TIDE

Chief Engineer on the trawler, Loch Ard in the late 1930s that sailed from Hull.

The ship and all her crew were never seen again, leaving Clara alone to bring up six children. Undaunted, she carried on working in the Joseph Rank flourmill, taking in washing and braiding fishing nets for the Kingston Steam Trawling Company.

As we were only in dock for three days and I hadn't yet arranged where to stay, Clara said 'There's a room here if you would like it.'

This I gladly accepted, not knowing that my first night in Hull would be the start of my forty years fishing and my new life in Hull.

Early next morning I decided to go on the market and see how the Kingston Chrysoberyl's fish was actually landed and sold and to get a better view of St Andrew's Dock in full daylight. I wandered down Hessle Road to Liverpool Street, over the bridge to where the Kingston Steam Trawling office was, then on to the market.

Here was a great hive of activity, the Kingston Chrysoberyl was landing her catch of White Sea plaice. The unloaders, who went by the name of 'Bobbers' were all over the ship. Basket after basket, full to the brim of plaice, were pulled up from the fish holds and emptied into butts called kits, each kit weighing ten stones. These kits were then lined up ready for sale. When the ship was empty the fish salesmen and buyers appeared and an auction took place. The sale was quickly concluded by which time each kit had a label on it, indicating which fish merchant had bought it.

The next thing that I was informed of was that I could obtain a fish pass from our firm's agent, which enabled me to get a free 'fry of plaice' and permitted me to take it off the dock.

As I wandered round St Andrew's Dock, taking in

Robert Baillie

all its operations, I was amazed by all the activity. Here was a dock totally alive with trawlers leaving, arriving, landing their fish, taking on coal and water stores. Trawlers under repair, being painted and preparing for sea.

A little later in the morning I saw hundreds of fishermen coming down the dock office from different firms to what was called 'settling day'. Here you were informed the amount of money that your voyage had made and what you were due to pick up. Each member of the crew being paid a share of the total voyage. This amounted to so many pounds to the thousand therefore the more thousands you made the bigger the cheque.

When I picked up my share I was quite happy with it. In fact it seemed a very good living. Then, to my amazement when I contacted my parents by telephone to tell them about the voyage, they informed me that during the month I was away, three registered envelopes had come from Kingston. It was only then that I found out that as well as the bonus called 'poundage', you were also on a weekly wage. Mine had been sent to my next of kin taken from the ship's log when I signed on for my first voyage.

My father, a true Scot, said, 'Boy, you've struck a Klondike.' I agreed and was ready to go on my next voyage as soon as possible…

After settling the crew were ready to make merry. They invited me to join them and we all made our way back to Hessle Road, the fishermen's road. Here was a line of their famous pubs, including Millars, Halfway, Criterion, and of course Rayners, the most famous of the Hessle Road pubs and a central meeting place of all the fishermen. Drinks? Well, they included Hull Brewery beers and another favourite Hull brew, the famous Lord Charles' Rum. This road was another hive of activity, with tills ringing in the shops, pubs full during the day with fishermen and clubs packed at night with fishermen and their wives and girlfriends.

A main routine on landing was the lads taking their wives and families shopping and then to the first house at Tivoli, for an evening of great stage entertainment with all top line stars. Then onto a pub singing room, such as Blue Heaven, Mayberry or the Dixon Arms for a night of great comradeship among the crews from all the fishing firms.

This was 1947 with great days and nights out and plenty of money flowing in the fishing fraternity. Yes, I'd hit a 'Klondike'.

After three days in Hull, it was sailing time again. So saying goodbye to Clara and phoning my parents in Scotland, I packed my bag again and set off back to the dock.

The original skipper, Sam Trolle was going back in Chrysoberyl. Sam was a Dane and a great old seaman. Him and I were going to sail together for quite a while. As I boarded this steam vessel for the second time I already felt a little more experienced in the fishing world.

I dumped my bag in my quarters and made my way straight to the bridge and there was old Sam. He didn't speak very good English and so with me with my Scots' accent the conversation wasn't that great. I introduced myself as the Radio Operator and old Sam looked at me a little puzzled. This was obviously something new to him, a radio officer?

Sam's seamanship went back to the sailing days. He was the proper mariner, so letting go we made our way out of dock and into the Humber, then to the Humber Light Vessel and onto Flamborough. But this voyage we were bound to Bear Island, so steaming NNE we passed Svino and then set a course for the

Robert Baillie

Arctic.

The last time that I'd sighted Bear Island had been from an aircraft while on patrol from the aircraft carrier on the Russian convoy.

Steaming steadily on we would then pick up the 200-fathom line and then 100-fathom line on our fishing chart banks?

Bear Island had a wireless telegraphy station, mainly for the metrology service, on medium frequency. The operator there would send at certain times his call sign LJB where this would enable us to take a D/F bearing to ascertain what bearing off Bear Island we were, fishing usually taking place on the SW – W – NW bearings. Here the fish was mostly cod and codling and there was plenty of it.

As it was November the first signs of minus temperatures and the dreaded NE gales and storms which brought even more severe freezing conditions were starting to appear.

Meanwhile I was getting to know Sam quite well. He usually just called me 'Scotsman'.

Sam's favourite drink was his pan of coffee that bubbled away continuously on the galley stove. Each cup was served with a generous dram of rum in it and was accompanied by a cigar. The cook usually brought this drink to the bridge and was invariably rewarded with a dram of his own. Not surprisingly, Sam got plenty of coffee brought to him!

We shot our gear on the SW bearing towing northerly to the W bearing and each time hauled in a really good catch of cod.

It was during this voyage that I was initiated into what was known as 'liver boiling'. As everyone on board worked for the voyage and to get extra money I was happy to join in this activity. This job entailed dragging baskets of livers, which the crew had gutted from the cod along the deck to the liver house on the starboard side aft.

The liver house had four boilers that were heated by steam. The livers were emptied into the boiler, the lid was shut down, the steam turned on and the livers boiled.

After a while the boilers were switched off and allowed to cool. The cod liver oil rose to the top and the sediment sank to the bottom. The oil ran off through filters into a tank, whilst the sediment ran into another. And we were paid on the number of barrels of oil that we produced.

The food was always something that I looked forward to on these voyages and the cook in his small galley worked wonders with what he had. It was wonderful to smell the freshly baked bread each day even though most of our meals of course naturally consisted of fish. Breakfast was usually fresh bread and fried fish, with cereals or porridge. Dinner was freshly made soup, potatoes and junk meat followed by currant pudding. Tea was stew and fried fish again. Supper was bread, corned beef and cold fish left over from tea. But there was plenty of it and after doing 18 hours on deck and six hours below, you were tired and hungry, so any meal was gladly accepted and you couldn't complain.

As the voyages went on my favourite crewman was without doubt the cook. And I certainly started to put weight on.

The voyage carried on, trawling day and night off Bear Island, pulling on board full nets of cod. Here I maintained radio watch for weather reports and checked our bearing by the radio direction finder. When Bear Island transmitted his signal for the first time we were experiencing northeast winds, bringing a very sharp drop in temperature as far down as minus 5° from the plus temperatures of the past few days when the winds had been S-SW. We had already had a gale warning so preparations were made that when it arrived, we would be ready.

When the wind increased rapidly, skipper Sam ordered that the trawl and gear should be brought on board and fully lashed up. When this was done, the procedure was to get the ship up head to wind and dodge the storm out. So with the gear on board and the crew below deck we prepared to dodge out. The wind increased to gale force 10 from the northeast, with temperatures dropping below freezing. The sea crashed on board and left a film of ice on our masts, rigging and railings. For two days we dodged the northeast wind, then fortunately it decreased, the seas dropped and the fishing resumed.

Remember that on this steamship, the crew were for'ard, so they had to come over the deck to get to the messrooms. This meant that the crew had to get storm-rigged in oilskins simply to get from for'ard to aft for meals or to come on watch.

Another very dangerous undertaking was getting a wash. As there were no baths or showers on board, the only way to wash was in a bucket. But we at least we found a unique way of getting some hot water. The boilers in the liver house were heated by steam, so by taking a boiler and heating it, we could get undressed, draw a bucket of hot water and get washed.

Getting from the boiler house over the deck and back to your quarters in minus temperatures was a he-man effort. But it was worth it just to have a wash in piping hot water.

So the trawling went on. With the firemen still shovelling tons of coal into the furnaces. The deck men gutting fish. The fishroom men stowing the catch away in the freezing cold ice rooms. And the engineers keeping the engines lubricated and answering the regular ring of the telegraph bell.

Day and night, this went on constantly.

After a number of days fishing, we had on board enough fish to go to market with. The gear was brought on board and stowed, the decks cleared and the fish rooms battened down. Only then were the crew free to go to their quarters. Most would go to sleep. A watch would come to the bridge, this made up of mate and two watchmen. Next the bosun with two watchmen and third hand with two watchmen taking different times during the twenty-four hours course SSW, then the skipper went below and finally myself.

I climbed into my small bunk and closed the two little doors and with the cabin warmed by the coal stove, sleep came quickly. After working 18 hours on and six hours below over the past few days and with the throb of the engines and the rise and fall of the ship, we were soon out for the count.

For four days we steamed SSW, passing Skomvaer and Svino, then into the North Sea and on to Flamborough. On the fifth day we passed Spurn, then once again anchored at the clock tower in Hull and waited for a landing number and tide time.

As soon as high water came, the dock gates opened, we entered St Andrew's Dock, moored up to the market side and all the engines stopped. The Bobbers were already there to board and prepare for landing as the crewmen carried their bags quickly ashore. I said cheerio to Sam and proceeded ashore, once again making my way to Hessle Road and my new home in Victoria Avenue...

Robert Baillie

CHAPTER 3
KINGSTON RUBY

On docking this time, Sam Trolle was informed that he was to take command of a bigger ship, the Kingston Ruby. He then asked me if I would sail with him as his radio operator and I was happy to accept his invitation.

It was now near to Christmas and Sam was not taking Kingston Ruby until after New Year, so here was my chance to go home for the Christmas holidays.

While on my two voyages my father had been upgraded to a higher class railway station as Stationmaster still in Fife in Scotland so off I went home but to a new home from when I first left to sail from Hull. It was a great re-union with my family and of course they had to listen to all my new sea yarns.

It was a great Christmas and New Year but immediately after I received a telegram to report back to Hull to sail in the Kingston Ruby. I returned to my Hull home and packed my bag once again.

'Cheerio Clara,' I said and off I went to the dock and signed on the Kingston Ruby. This trawler was much bigger and better equipped radio-wise. But as I boarded the vessel I saw that my small room had a bunk but little else. I checked the radio room and to my surprise it contained a rather modern transmitter with radiotelephone facilities, a battery box outside and two receivers, plus D/F on the bridge.

There was also a new device on the port side, a small direction finder that could detect all conversations on radio and find their bearing. I thought this was the greatest - skippers conversing where they were catching fish. And a quick 'snap' on this set and you had a bearing of them relating to your vessel.

WAITING FOR THE TIDE

The next surprise on the starboard side was a new depth sounder. Previously to get the sea bottom depth you had to switch on and read a flash along a graded scale, then switch off. But this new sounder was far more sophisticated.

It recorded the depth of the seabed at regular intervals and relayed them onto a roll of paper impregnated with an iodine-type solution, to produce a continuous brown contour line of the depth of the seabed. When I demonstrated the machine to Sam he nearly had a fit when he saw what the sea bottom looked like.

Soon we had let go and proceeded as usual to the Humber. This time we were bound to the Norwegian Coast fishing grounds – Andenes, Malangen, northwest banks where normally cod were here to spawn around Andenes. Here was a different fishing technique. Very strong currents prevailed along this coast so we towed one way all day and then steamed back to our starting position. Old Sam was a master here.

We commenced fishing at Andenes, using it as a starting position and a point that we could steam back to. Here was where I got plenty of watchkeeping and steering work.

The cod here were large and had huge livers with plenty of oil. This was also a spawning area, so we had the roe, which we made into roe paste, a delicacy and a supplement to our food.

The weather was a problem as regular low-pressure areas travelling northeast across the area resulted in some very stormy conditions and high seas. As we were steaming back huge seas would break over the bows and swamp the fish pounds where the crew were working gutting the fish. And if the winds were in a direction giving minus temperatures the seas were freezing. You can imagine what it was like working 18 hours a day in these conditions. The crew were freezing, wet and tired but they worked on and with plenty of fish around we were soon full up with both fish and cod liver oil.

Then once again, after quite a few days fishing we were bound for home. We steamed close to the Norwegian Coast and passed Skomvaer, then down to Svino and through the North Sea until at last we anchored at the clock tower and again waited for the tide. Here we had a wash down with a bucket of warm water and combed our hair for probably the first time in days, then changed into our shore clothes.

Life seemed great.

Once back in dock I made my way to my second home. But after greetings to Clara and a brief description of the voyage it was time to get changed and get back to the dock. Although most jobs were completed at sea, there were still a couple of radio repairs and various bits and pieces for me to clear up.

Marconi employed most of the radio officers on the trawlers but I was employed directly by the Kingston Steam Trawler Company, so I had to report to Kingston's secretary concerning anything required for the next voyage. He was a Mr Carnes, a very capable man and a gentleman who was going to play a big part in my future years with the firm.

Well, it was settling time again. We had sold the full voyage so a reasonable cheque was obtained. One thing with Kingstons was that we were paid with a Barclay's cheque, which meant a quick trip off the dock to Barclay's Bank on Boulevard. And as a true Scot, most of it was banked with the remainder kept for the time in dock. Then it was back home for dinner before the usual trip round Hessle Road for a drink with the crew.

Old Sam Trolle's 'headquarters' pub was the

WAITING FOR THE TIDE

'Halfway' near where he lived in Edinburgh Street. But Sam travelled to many places round the city and I had quite a merry time with him on several occasions.

The trawler radio officers' main pub was the 'Wheatsheaf', not far from the Marconi's Percy Street office and the Radio Officers' Union building. This was my first 'sightseeing' tour of Hull. But after only three days in dock it was sailing time again. There was never much time at home and for leisure but this I soon realised was 'the fishing life'.

I boarded Kingston Ruby once more, this time bound for Bear Island. And about five days later we arrived there and prepared to fish. The fishing was pretty slack and we observed for the first time slush ice passing us the more northerly that we went. Then in the distance we saw actual ice floes. We had now got round on the East bearing but still fishing was poor. This time at the island we even considered steaming to the White Sea.

During my watch on the radio listening for fishing information, I was astounded to hear two skippers talking and by their conversation they were catching plenty of fish. But where was their position?

I went onto the bridge and informed Sam what I'd overheard. He agreed that this was great news as the fishing where we were was very slack. Our next move was to take a snap bearing, which indicated that the two skippers were to the east of us. Sam immediately got his gear on board and off we steamed to the east.

It was very calm but suddenly down came a fog bank. Our visibility was cut to a few yards but we steamed on at a reduced speed, but then crunch! We were in the ice!

So here it was. Thick fog and an ice field! We stopped and floated with the ice in the fog.

Then, as quickly as it had arrived the fog cleared.

Robert Baillie

We could see the ice but also in view was the island called Sea Horse. But there was no sight of the two trawlers that were catching the fish. Patiently we waited for the two skippers to speak again. Soon they were back on talking and a quick snap with our D/F showed that they were still to the east of us. Eventually we sighted them. I imagine they were not only surprised to see us but were also very curious about how we had found them.

We shot our trawl and then hauled after a towing period. And there it was – a trawl full of cod. Sam was delighted because on this position we caught a full voyage. It was then that the importance of the radio operator became apparent and the beginning of skipper and radio operator being together for quite some time.

Through this co-operation many a full ship of fish was caught, not by the skill of the skipper but by how the radio operator was able to pick up information and direct a skipper to a position. This was proved on this voyage and many subsequent voyages during my time at sea.

After several days fishing we had a full ship and it was time to set off again for home. This time though with care, as we had to navigate round the ice field. One of the more memorable and wonderful sights was to see the Leopard Seals on the ice floes, floating slowly passed our vessel with their cubs lazily looking at us…

On entering the dock I was informed by Mr Carnes that Sam Trolle was going in the Kingston Pearl for one voyage. I would go with him but this would be our last voyage together as I was being transferred to the Kingston Diamond on my return with skipper John Moore.

So I sailed in the Kingston Pearl with Sam on our last trip. Sam and I had sailed together for one and a half years. This voyage was back to the Malangen Bank, off the Norwegian coast, where we got quite a good catch.

When we returned to dock, Sam and I went for a drink and a final farewell. Sam was without doubt one of the greatest old seamen I had the pleasure to sail with.

After my last trip with Sam, I took stock of the skippers who I sailed with at Kingstons. They included Bill Cornish, Charlie Hogg, Billy Hornby, Jack Moore, Squib Evans, Tommy Lowrie, Dan Upson and Bob McCullogh, who was known as 'Stormy Bob' as he never used to know what bad weather was and towed in all sorts of storms and gales.

Another skipper who I will never forget was Jimmy Shaugnessey - The Bear Island Ghost – and the only skipper who could bring a voyage of codlings home and sell them when others were left unsold on the market.

The Kingston Diamond was one of the larger steam trawlers holding much more fish than the rest. I went aboard it to have a look round. The radio room was more modern with a better transmitter and receivers. It also had a new type of direction finder, which had no rotating loop but a fixed twin loop (Bellini Tossi) and a set in the radio room with a dial and compass card.

On the bridge the equipment was also a bit more modern with an echo depth sounder and a fish finder D/F on the port side. It was also now where the sending and receiving of telegrams 'shore to ship' and 'ship to shore' was available. The main coast stations were Humber Radio, Cullercoats Radio and Stonehaven Radio and our main station for communication shore to ship for all arctic trawlers was Wick Radio in the north of Scotland. We could now send and receive telegrams at sea and this of course meant we had a much closer contact with our firm and was a great boost to the trawler crews and their families.

I met my new skipper Jack Moore who was a top line Faroe fisherman and one of the youngest men to get his skipper's ticket. He was a tubby, dapper little individual but had the authority and the voice of a much bigger man who you always paid attention to.

We sailed for Bear Island on our first trip but later on we would be sailing together to Iceland and Greenland.

It was the normal procedure, west of Bear Island towing up to the north to the famous northwest gully.

There wasn't a great deal of fish here but reports that we received indicated that there was plenty up at Spitzbergen, so we steamed there. Here was a land frozen over in the winter and with plenty of pack ice still around in the Spring but there was definitely some good fishing here.

Jack changed the rules, working 19 hours on deck and 5 hours below. His reasoning for this was that if you were doing all these hours daily you were landing a lot of fish, so your time on the fishing grounds was reduced. Eventually we had enough fish to go to market, so set a SSW course back to Hull.

Now we could send telegrams, first to our firm with our time of arrival and the amount of the catch, then to the crew's families on when we would be arriving home. It was great to have a better transmitter and using Morse Code the telegrams were soon dispatched to Wick Radio. In turn Wick Radio had timely traffic lists, sending out all the ship's call signs that he had telegrams for. This was a twenty-four hour a day service, keeping us in touch with the world. These telegrams were of course highly confidential and the operator had the responsibility for maintaining this.

Kingston Diamond and skipper Jack Moore was

certainly a good combination for making good earnings. Every voyage, mostly to Bear Island was successful. We had done quite a few voyages there, when at the end of 1948, we were informed that Kingston Diamond would be coming out of fishing operations for a few months, as she was going to be converted from coal-fired to fired by fuel.

She was going to be the first trawler to be converted to oil fuel, no more coal and no more firemen shovelling it into the furnaces. The ship was going to Wallsend to be converted and the skipper and I would be ashore until it was finished.

I also learned that the Diamond was going to be fitted with radar and would be the first trawler in Hull with it. For those not acquainted with radar this was a device that had a revolving parabolic aerial that transmitted and received signals of a very high frequency. The signal when transmitted would be reflected back to the aerial and then to an indicator on the bridge. This indicator looked like a large dial with an electronic sweep line going round in a circle in synchronisation with the revolving aerial. Each target hit with this beam would come on the dial as a white spot of light. We could now look at the coastline, ships, buoys etc, even in dense fog.

As I was ashore for a while, I went home to Scotland to visit my family. Whilst I had been away my father had been promoted again to a higher position as Stationmaster at Buckhaven in Fife.

As the Kingston Diamond was going to be fitted with radar I decided to enrol at Leith Nautical College in Edinburgh and on January 24 1949 I entered the college to commence a radar course. Each morning at 08.00 I travelled by train from Buckhaven to Edinburgh and returned each night at 18.00 over the famous Forth Rail Bridge. Then there was just time for dinner, a little

Robert Baillie

No. **480**

RADAR OBSERVER
ON
MERCHANT SHIPS

This is to certify that

NAME   ROBERT BAILLIE

RANK   RADIO OFFICER

CERTIFICATE OF
COMPETENCY, GRADE 2nd Cl. P.M.G.   NO.   c/9657   DISCHARGE BOOK NO.   -

DATE AND PLACE OF BIRTH 8th September 1924   -   JEDBURGH.

completed a course of training in Radar Observation, approv
by the Ministry of Transport, held from 24th January   *19*
to 4th February   *19*49 , *at*   LEITH NAUTICAL COLLEGE
                                          (NAME OF SCHOOL)
and passed the examination held by the School Authorities
the conclusion of the course.

                   Signed   *[signature]*
                                        (INSTRUCTOR OF COURSE)

                   Signed   *[signature]*
                                          (PRINCIPAL OF SCHOOL)

Signature of Holder   *[signature]*   *Date*   4/2/49

(62820) W: 43744/840 10 Pads 2/47 H J R & L G

book study and bed. Then up again at 6am to catch the train for another 9 o'clock start at college.

During my stay at home I received an enquiry from Mr Carnes asking what I was doing?

I informed him that I was studying at Leith Nautical College for my radar certificate. May I point out that when you came out of a ship you were off all earnings, so all my college fees were paid out of my savings, which I had accumulated during my fishing voyages.

Later, after obtaining my radar certificate I had a telegram to state Kingston Diamond was ready and to proceed to Wallsend. I said cheerio to my parents and my brother and sister and proceeded to Wallsend.

When I arrived at the dock, there was Diamond all fitted out and freshly painted. I went aboard and up onto the bridge. My radio room had been converted to hold the radar equipment, and a new transmitter and receiver, and a radar indicator had been fitted.

As I looked around the ship, I thought there's something strange here, no black, belching smoke from the funnel. Making my way aft and down to the engine room, here was the answer – gleaming new pipes and boilers etc. We were now fired by oil, how clean it all looked.

Skipper Jack Moore and the crew arrived. We let go and with a pilot guiding us, came slowly out to the Tyne entrance. We dropped the pilot and steamed down the coast towards Flamborough.

I switched on the radar and stared at the amazing 'picture' of the coastline and ships etc. I remember Jack was astounded at how the images were produced on the radar screen so accurately.

We arrived at Hull and moored up and I was informed that Mr Carnes wanted to see me. I went straight to his office and he asked me about my college

Robert Baillie

course, how much it had cost and what other expenses I had incurred?

When I gave him the details he informed me that Kingstons had decided as I had gone to college to take a 'radar' certificate that was also in their interest, I was to get all my fees, expenses and my weekly wages while at college reimbursed to me.

He took me down to the cashier and I received a cheque. I looked at it and thought this indeed is another Klondike. I then quickly left the dock and proceeded straight to Barclays Bank on the Boulevard.

We sailed again, this time on an oiled-fired ship and fitted with radar. Proceeding down the Humber, the radar showed the entire river coastline and most importantly the buoys. What an asset this was going to be in thick fog and snow. We steamed steadily to Svino in Norway and then once again up the Norwegian coast to Lodingen with my new transmitter which was of a higher power and had more radio frequency ranges on it.

I contacted Roervik Radio by Morse and sent out our ETA to the pilot station at Lodingen. Then, picking up the Pilot we made our way through the fiords to Honningsvag. The Pilot was greatly impressed with our radar that showed even the smallest of buoys during our passage through the fiords.

Arriving at Honningsvag, we dropped the pilot and made our way out, passing Nord Kyn and steaming east. We decided to shoot our trawl outside the limit line off Tana fiord.

With our radar we could position ourselves very accurately. This was most essential when working the limit line, which was a line on our chart following the coastline and indicating the Norwegian fishing limit. You were not allowed to fish inside this line that was patrolled regularly by Norwegian gunboats. If you were caught inside it, you were arrested and could get your catch and gear confiscated and receive a very hefty fine.

When we had towed for a while, we hauled our net in and saw that it was loaded with fish. The most remarkable thing was that we were the only trawler around. Soon our deck was full and we had to stop fishing and lay while the crew started gutting the fish. This could take quite a few hours. Meanwhile with our radar we could keep our exact position where we had caught our fish, it was a great machine…

While layed gutting the fish, a small Norwegian fishing boat came alongside us. On board there was a skipper and a crew of four. The skipper requested to come on board and Jack agreed.

The Norwegian skipper then asked Jack if he could have the small fish that we were throwing overboard and use it as bait for his kreels.

In return he and his crew would come on board and assist with the gutting. Five extra men would be a godsend and so again Jack readily agreed. The Norwegians came on board and all day gutted the fish and in return our lads filled their baskets full of small fish. They then departed into Tana Fiord and returned the next morning.

This went on for three days.

Each time we hauled, our deck was full and with the extra help, we were soon full up. We departed leaving our little Norwegian boat full of small fish.

We then sailed back to Honningvaag, then to Lodingen, up the west fiord and a course for home with a very good catch.

However, the crunch came when we docked in Hull and Jack was informed that he was on a charge!

He was accused of exporting fish into a foreign country and also of employing foreign labour, both without a licence. We found out that the Norwegian

Kingston Diamond

skipper had taken the fish that we had given him to use as bait but had in fact sold it ashore. Fortunately this was later resolved much to Jack's delight.

The catch fetched good money, a success that was mainly due to our new radar enabling us to fish a bit closer to the limit line, which before had always been a bit of a gamble. But after this success, our next voyage, to Iceland, promised to be something very different.

I couldn't wait...

Meanwhile at home, I had become much more settled at Clara's. Instead of being just a lodger I was beginning to feel more like part of the family. Two sons and a daughter remained at home and although I did not spend a great amount of time there, I started to get to know them more and more. The only problem was that my Scots' accent seemed to hold me back when I was in conversation with them. Rita, in particular would often look at me curiously when I talked to her and it was disappointing to think that she might not understand me very well.

It was soon nearing summer. We sailed for Iceland on the same departure route; River Humber, Spurn and Flamborough but now we were going to sail up the east coast of England and Scotland. We passed Scarborough and The Tyne, then up the coast to Kinnairds Head, then a course to Duncansby Head, through the Pentland Firth and passed the Faroe Islands. We had decided to make for the southwest coast of Iceland and a course was set to bring us to the Vestmann Islands, then to Reykjanesta and across Faxafloi to a position off Snaefellsjokull. This area was widely known to fishermen as 'Snowy'.

On later voyages Iceland looked a sinister land, covered by vast, white mountains, many of them volcanic. But now, the snow and ice was thawing and the scenery appeared quite different.

Joe Lofts, Knobby North and I on Kingston Diamond in 1947

WAITING FOR THE TIDE

Iceland was smack in the way of all low-pressure areas travelling northeast, which could give horrendous weather conditions with sub zero temperatures. Later in my career I would experience these conditions and the terrible toll that they took of both men and ships.

We picked up Snaefellsjokull and with the help of our radar decided to tow across the face of a glacier, keeping a distance outside the limit line. We shot our trawl and after a short time hauled in the net. It contained a stupendous catch of beautiful Icelandic fish, which according to the fish merchants in Hull was superior and much sought after.

This was great. By maintaining our position accurately by radar we mustered a great voyage. The weather remained fine and we were quickly on our way home again. Jack Moore was extremely pleased and as he was predominantly a Bear Island man, he regarded this voyage as a real bonus.

We docked in Hull and had no problem selling the fish and making quite a handsome amount of money. Once again, as a Scotsman who had left his homeland to earn a pound, I thought I had definitely picked the right place…

The remainder of our voyages in Kingston Diamond were to Bear Island. Meanwhile two brand new, oil-fired ships had joined Kingstons, Kingston Sardius commanded by Bill Cornish and Kingston Peridot commanded by Charlie Hogg.

Also being built were another two, the first of the three-bridge type, Kingston Topaz and Kingston Garnet.

Both the skippers from the Sardius and Peridot were going to be moved up. Jack Moore was informed that he would be taking Kingston Sardius later and I would be moving with him, so we both had a spell in dock waiting for the Sardius.

During my last voyage in Kingston Diamond we had a new bosun join us, another Scotsman named John Neilsen. He and I struck up a friendship being the only two Scotsmen on board in a crew made up mainly of Yorkshiremen.

While waiting for Sardius I did one voyage in Kingston Peridot with Charles Hogg as skipper, Arthur Moss as mate and Percy Bell as bosun. These three men were going to play a big part in my future career...

WAITING FOR THE TIDE

CHAPTER 4
A DAY AT THE RACES

Meanwhile back home in Wellstead Street, we were enjoying some beautiful warm weather. During our stay in dock we relied on a taxi service to get us around and I had a permanent fellow, Billy Burke, who usually ran me around. On this particular sunny day, it was also Beverley Races and Bill asked me, 'Are we going to the races?'

It seemed a good idea so I quickly went home to change and Bill said that he would call to pick me up an hour later. When I got home I was surprised to see that Rita, Clara's daughter, was there. She informed me that it was her day off, so hoping that she would now understand what I was saying, I asked her, 'With it being such a beautiful, sunny day, would you like to come to Beverley Races?'

I was very pleased when she replied that she would love to go, so when Bill called to pick me up, I informed him that there was now three of us going. So off we went to enjoy a fantastic day out in the sunshine. It was my first time at Hull's local racetrack and was quite different from wandering around the freezing Arctic…

Whilst I was in Hull waiting to join Kingston Sardius I caught up a little more with the huge amount of new technical innovations that were being introduced into our industry. Many of these were concerned with navigation and echo sounding and had appeared or were going to appear in the near future and would greatly affect the fishing industry and its ships. Most of these new navigational aids were associated with radio waves. First we encountered the consol. This was simply two stations, one at Bushmills in Ireland, the other at Stavanger in Norway that would emit a series of dashes and dots. You simply tuned your receiver to each station in turn, then counted whichever came first, the dashes or dots, until you heard them fade away, and noted the count. A specially prepared chart was available with dashes and dots and by applying your count to this chart from both stations, a position was found.

A more accurate instrument came along called 'Loran', which was short for long-range navigation. Here once again you had two stations, positioned in different countries. A master signal was transmitted followed a short time later by a slave signal and on an indicator you could read the time difference between the master and slave arriving at your ship. Another chart was available with the time differences printed on it, which once again allowed you to chart your position by reading the time differences obtained from the two stations.

Another device was the Decca Navigator. With this device, radio transmissions from three different stations were read off on a special instrument containing three clock-face dials in three different colours. You simply read off a reading on each dial, applied it to a special Decca Chart of similar colour and where your three readings intersected was your position.

Echo sounders had also developed and now as well as reading sea depths, you could also actually record and track the movement of fish shoals. This new advancement was undoubtedly going to revolutionis future fishing operations.

The Kingston Sardius arrived home and after it had landed its catch we took it over. It was a fine, oil-fired vessel with modern transmitters and receivers. My radio room was a lot bigger than on the Diamond with a comfortable bunk that I could actually walk around. One great thing about oil-fired ships was that they were clean, with no coal dust hanging about.

The radar had a longer range and the echo sounders were very advanced.

We were informed that Sardius would do two voyages and then undergo a survey.

In a few days we were ready, so off we sailed for Bear Island. And as it was mid-summer, it was pleasant sailing.

Jack Moore liked his music, in fact his codeword on his telegram's ship to shore address read 'Musical Hull' and there was a link from the radio room to a small speaker in his cabin for his piped music.

Fishing at Bear Island was pretty slack at this time of year but up at Spitzbergen it was reasonable. You could encounter ice floes the further north you went but it was usually quite pleasant fishing around this area. My friend John Neilsen had joined as bosun and it was fine having another Scot aboard. As usual Jack Moore had caught a voyage and although it took a bit longer to catch than usual we were quite happy with it, so we steamed for home. It was a fine passage back to Hull, where we anchored off the clock tower and waited for the tide and time.

On docking we were informed that a dry dock was available for Sardius and that we would stop for a survey which would probably be over a period of three weeks.

'Dry docking' meant the ship's bottom was scraped of all barnacles and was then painted and the propeller etc overhauled. So with this news I decided to go home to Scotland for a holiday.

When I arrived at my home in Wellstead Street, Rita, Clara's daughter was also on holiday. She

Robert Baillie

informed me that she wasn't going anywhere, so once again I asked her, 'Would you like to come to Scotland?'

After a long pause she replied, Yes! She would come to Scotland with me. And that was it. I telephoned my parents, then packed my case and we were on the next train and off on holiday...

When we arrived in Buckhaven, Scotland, the weather was bright and sunny. My parents and five brothers and one sister welcomed Rita and so started a very enjoyable spell of leave, away from the stressful times spent in the Arctic. We visited the city of Edinburgh, toured the East Fife resorts and various other places of interest. It certainly was a fine holiday but all too soon it came to an end and we returned to Hull.

It was then that we struck up a close relationship with John Neilsen, our bosun and his wife Joan. As a foursome we attended all the great functions of that time; The Bombers' Ball, The Skippers and Mates' Ball, The Lord Mayor of Hull's Ball, The Hull City Police Ball, The Hull Mail Ball and various others that all had top line bands playing. We also visited other popular venues of the time including Tivoli, Blue Heaven and the Mayberry Singing Rooms.

As 1949 drew to a close, the Sardius had completed her survey and was ready to sail again. I looked forward to my first trip in this more comfortable version of the ship.

A new era for the radio operator was about to begin. The competition in the fishing world was becoming much greater. New and bigger trawlers were being introduced and the trawler firms were demanding more from their skippers. The skipper's career hinged on him being able to come home with a full ship and in a short time, voyage after voyage. You could always fill a ship if you were away long enough, but the fish merchants were looking for short voyages with fresh fish. If one ship was away for an eighteen-day voyage and another for twenty-eight days, the merchants would naturally always prefer the shorter one.

The Arctic was a vast place and for a skipper to find the best fishing grounds using only his own intuition and experience, no matter how good that may be, was almost impossible.

It was vital when he sailed that he had up to the minute information of where the fish was. And here is where the radio operator came in. A good operator could make a good skipper into a very good one, just by being conscientious, hard-working and gleaning twenty-four hours a day fishing information from the fishing grounds.

When we sailed again in the Sardius to the Arctic fishing grounds, November was upon us and around Bear Island we started to experience the stormy northeast winds with zero temperatures. These conditions would deteriorate further as the months went on. Months when there was no daylight, just endless night. Months when the ships were covered with ice and the trawls had to be hosed down with hot water. When the winches had to be freed of ice before operating them. And when the radar stopped working and I had to climb on top of the bridge to chip the ice off the aerials before I could transmit anything. Months when even the steam pipes to the cod liver oil plant had to be thawed out. When virtually everything on board was frozen.

The fishermen worked for eighteen hours a day on the open deck in these cruel conditions, their hands frozen and the ice-cold sea crashing around them in the continuous darkness.

I often wondered about the shoreman as he sat down to eat his fish and chips, probably complaining

Kingston Sardius

about the extra hour he had to do at work that day.

Did he realise what the fishermen had to go through to get that fish onto his table?

I doubted it!

We sailed on as Christmas and the New Year came and went. And as we battled against the icy Arctic, still hundreds of miles from home, we thought of our loved ones...

1950 was a very special and memorable year for me. I got engaged to Rita early in the year and we planned to get married in the December, when we estimated that Sardius would be in dock again for another survey.

During the year as Rita and I made plans for the wedding, I often recalled my first voyage on Kingston Chrysoberyl in 1947, when the first deckhand to come aboard had been George White, Rita's brother. What a fateful meeting that had proved to be. And now, only three years later, Rita and I were getting married. It all seemed like a fairytale but it was true.

We sailed in the Sardius throughout 1950. The year seemed to fly by as we traversed and fished nearly every area in the Arctic Ocean including Bear Island, Spitzbergen, the White Sea, the Norwegian Coast and Iceland. And before I had the chance to realise it, the time for another survey was approaching and so was the wedding.

We arrived back in Hull in early December and were informed that a dry dock had been booked for Sardius' survey for January 1951. A dry dock was a special dock that a ship could sail into. The dock gates were opened, the ship sailed in and the gates were closed again. Then the water was pumped out, the ship was allowed to drop down on a special cradle and was propped up so that workers could clean the bottom of the ship and check the propellers etc. When the work

had been completed the dock was filled again, the gates were opened and the ship sailed out. So with everything sorted out regarding my ship, it was time to complete my wedding arrangements.

The wedding date had been arranged for December 23 1950. Rita and I were to be married in St Nicholas' Church on Hessle High Road and the best man was to be my good friend John Neilsen, the bosun of the Sardius.

I went up to Moore & Robsons, Hull Brewery. We had booked the church hall next to St Nicholas' Church for the reception and evening entertainment. Moore & Robsons provided the catering, so the tables, food, drinks and even the glasses were all supplied by them and set up in the hall. The next thing I needed was a band, so I booked The Hull Yeomanry Dance Band to provide the entertainment.

Our wedding day finally arrived and we were married in St Nicholas' Church with a 'full regalia' service, which included choirboys.

My parents, brothers and sister, Rita's family and all her friends and Jack Moore and his wife were in attendance. The celebrations lasted until midnight in the church hall. It was certainly a day to remember. And as it was also Christmas and New Year, the celebrations continued throughout the festive season. John, Joan, Rita and I had a hectic but very enjoyable week that none of us would ever forget…

At the start of 1951, the Sardius had completed her survey and was nearly ready for another voyage. So once again we went aboard to start the normal routine of checking the radio equipment, stores and spares etc.

The ship getting stored up with food, fuel, ice for the fish rooms, fresh water and fishing gear including spare nets, net mending twine, bobbins and warps, there

Mending nets in heavy weather - 1950s

was an endless itinerary.

In mid January we set sail for Bear Island. We should actually have been going to the Norwegian coast to fish as the weather conditions around Bear Island were at their worst during this month. We heard though that the merchants had been receiving only the big fish from the Norwegian and were looking for some codlings. This made our minds up to go to Bear Island.

We steamed north-northeast as usual, passing Skomvaer in Norway and making our way to Bear Island. On arrival we found that we were seemingly the only trawler there. As we approached the SW bearing the wind changed to the northeast and started to increase Then within an hour or so was up to force 6-7 and worse still, the temperature dropped rapidly to below zero. The wind continued to increase further until in the end we had to dodge northeast with a howling gale around us.

Quickly we started to ice up. The masts, riggings, deck rails, decks and the bridge and finally the radar equipment iced up and was no longer usable and often there was no way that you could get out to clear them.

For nearly four days we dodged northeast, getting heavier and heavier with ice. Our windows blocked up with ice and we couldn't see out. It was a precarious position. Thankfully on the fourth day the northeast wind started to decrease and moved to the southwest. I was able to get out and go on top of the bridge to free the radar aerial. While I was up there the moon came out and I looked around. To my amazement I sighted pack ice ahead and around us on both sides. I quickly scrambled back down and informed Jack. I switched on the radar and there it was - an icefield.

We slowly came round and went back southwest clear of it. Then after the crew had cleared the ice from the ship, we shot our gear. When we hauled we had a

Greenland - 1950s

trawlful of codling and in quick time we had a full voyage. We set off home still keeping the southwest wind and now clear of ice. We arrived off the clock tower to be informed that the Merchants were clamouring for our voyage. We docked immediately and I set off for home. Rita and I had a room at her mother's until we got our own house a little later.

The next day, I went down to the dock to 'settle' and was met with the great news that our voyage had netted £10,000 – a Klondike!

1951 was another year that passed by very quickly as we steamed many hundreds of miles and fished many of the Arctic fishing grounds.

The year was also one where the fishing industry continued to move ahead at a steady pace. We were leaving the days of steam and ships with no running water or baths, with toilets on the open deck, washing ourselves down with a bucket of water, paraffin lamps and fish rooms loaded with coal, far behind.

Kingstons had already moved ahead. After Sardius and Peridot, the new trawlers had come along Garnet and Zircon, with three bridges, although I always thought that these two vessels looked very similar to Peridot and Sardius but with an extra bridge.

Robert Baillie

CHAPTER 5
I'M A SPY

The next of the new-look breed of vessels to be launched included the Kingston Jacinth and in recognition of his service and moneymaking voyages, Jack Moore was informed that he would be taking this new ship. It was due to arrive in town dock in the near future and most of the crew from the Sardius would be joining it. We bid goodbye to the Sardius, a truly great ship and waited for the Jacinth.

When I boarded the Jacinth, a proper three-bridge ship, there was nothing I could do but look around in amazement.

My quarters were on the middle deck of the bridge area, next door to the Captain's and consisted of a brand new cabin with a bunk, a table and a cushioned seat.

I then explored the rest of the deck that comprised of the officers' mess room, the mate's cabin, the bosun's cabin and a small pantry with a sink and running hot and cold water. Then there was a bathroom. Yes, there it was, a bathroom with a bath and an indoor toilet! Through the alleyway to aft, there was the galley and the crew's messroom and quarters. Then up on the bridge was my radio room, fitted by Redifon, a new company in the fishing industry. Here were the most modern transmitters and receivers, a Loran navigation set and the most up to date echo sounders and D/Fs. And in what was termed the day room was a chart table and radar.

This was luxury compared to what we had sailed on before. We had our trials in the River Humber where one of our guests was the great footballer Raich Carter who played for Hull City during the team's glory days...

WAITING FOR THE TIDE

Our maiden voyage was to Bear Island, Greenland. This modern trawler had everything; good speed, excellent manoeuvrability and handling and plenty of fish space.

We left Hull bound for Greenland. The funny thing that I remember about the trip was that although we were steaming west in the Atlantic, the skipper's ticket only allowed us to go to a certain longitude, passed which we had to have a navigator on board. This rule was changed later on but on this voyage we still had to take one.

Our navigator was an old, retired merchant navy captain but I'm afraid that having a dram or two was more of a pastime for him than navigating. But anyway, off we sailed, up to the Pentland Firth, then making our way westerly and passing the last bit of mainland, the Butt of Lewis, I checked the Loran navigator and it was okay.

We continued into the North Atlantic and westerly, making for Cape Farewell, Greenland. The voyage westerly was mainly overcast, cloudy weather, so no sun was observed and therefore no sextant reading was possible. As a result there was no need for our navigator up to now.

We checked our position by Loran but this was only good to a certain longitude. Where we left the British stations there was a dead space before we picked up the western stations. Cape Farewell had a transmitting signal that was emitted at intervals allowing you to take a D/F bearing, which was very helpful.

The first hint of the trouble ahead was when we sighted a large number of icebergs floating around. Then suddenly we saw it. Pack ice!

We could see the mountains of Greenland and eventually picked up Cape Farewell on our radar but

Robert Baillie

night had fallen and in the darkness we got further and further into the ice. The wind increased and we had to stop, trapped in the ice and battered by a strong wind. Things had got a bit serious.

The rise and fall of the ice field seemed to be crunching us heavily with ice piling up on our port side and threatening to come on board. The thought was that if we started our engine, would the ice damage our propeller?

Under the circumstances we had to move and try to get round on the opposite course to the one that we had entered the ice field on. We came round at a very slow speed and proceeded on the opposite course until we glided into clear water.

When daylight came we were certainly in clear water but we only had a small clearance. We were still surrounded by ice but in the daylight we could see a narrow opening through the ice field, so we slowly steamed through it. We cleared the field and then took stock of what damage we had incurred in the ice, especially to our port side where the ice had piled up.

We realised that we couldn't steam very far so we followed the ice pack round and got into a position off a small bank near Julianehab, clear of the ice pack.

Here we got a very good voyage of Greenland cod and then set off home again across the North Atlantic, once again through the Pentland Firth, the North Sea, passed Spurn and into Hull. As we came alongside the dock entrance, portside to the dock master, he informed us in no uncertain terms, 'Your port side is in a bit of a mess!'

Needless to say we required some new plates as they had been rubbed thin by the pack ice.

Our second voyage to Greenland was again to Cape Farewell. This time the pack ice had cleared but there were still numerous small icebergs known as 'growlers' around.

It was during this voyage that the fishing fraternity in Hull suffered its first Greenland tragedy - the loss of the trawler, Norman.

The majority of ships were fishing near to Cape Farewell. The routine was to fish in daylight and lay at night because of icebergs. While the crew and skipper were snatching some sleep I was on watch on the bridge keeping a radar watch and lookout while we were laid.

In the early hours of the morning, whilst watching the radar I observed an object moving slowly towards the rocks. Now as a small iceberg drifting slowly could be mistaken for a ship and likewise a ship of trawler size, moving slowly could be mistaken for a small berg.

Just as I had noticed the object there was a shout on the radio, 'Look out! There's a ship moving close to the rocks.'

The next thing we knew was that the Norman had run aground on the rocks. He must have gashed his keel. The crew it was assumed had got off the ship but had in fact been swept away by the heavy currents.

It was treacherous around Cape Farewell. The rocks were numerous but were not charted very well. For another trawler to attempt to go in there to help would have been suicide and undoubtedly have caused the loss of more lives.

Later the Norman slid off the rock and sank. Debris was washed up and bodies were picked up by other trawlers in the area and brought home. There was only one survivor. By an act of God he had been washed up on another rock and was saved. And by coincidence he was also named Norman.

We once again had caught a voyage but Greenland was going to give us another shock. While leaving the area in the dark there was a deafening thud. The shock sent a shudder through the ship and we

Robert Baillie

stopped and once again laid in the dark.

Daylight saw us in an area where lots of large growlers were floating around. We must have hit one of them. We checked our bow and down the focsle and anchor chain locker and as there was no apparent leakage it was full steam ahead for home. Fortunately we arrived in Hull with no serious damage.

We sailed with Jacinth for quite a while after that, mostly to Bear Island but after one trip Jack Moore announced that he was stopping ashore. He planned to start a fruit and veg shop in Hull!

This was a sad moment for me as Jack and I had sailed many miles and oceans together. So just as it had been with Sam Trolle, it was time for another goodbye.

There was another unforgettable episode that happened aboard the Jacinth as we steamed to Spitzbergen under a new skipper who was taking the ship for just one voyage.

On August 17 1952 while passing Cape Bull, Bear Island en route to Spitzbergen I received a telegram. My wife Rita had given birth to our first child, a daughter who we named Patricia Jean. So it was out with the whisky and a dram all round to the crew.

Various skippers took Jacinth during my remaining time on her, the last one before I moved ships was Norman Trolle, one of Sam Trolle's sons. We went to Iceland fishing at the North Cape in wild, stormy weather and freezing conditions. We caught a voyage, which on our return to Hull netted £9,000!

James Shaugnessy was going to take Jacinth and I was going in Kingston Garnet with Norman Trolle. So it was a final goodbye to my 'new' ship the Kingston Jacinth and for a short period I sailed in the Kingston Garnet before transferring to the Kingston Emerald.

During the whole of 1953 I sailed in the Garnet with Norman Trolle. We did quite well, working outside the limit line mostly on the North Norwegian coast between Nord Kynn and Vardo.

By January 1954 I had saved enough money to buy our new house. Rita and I bought one in Cambridge Road, Hessle, which at the time was known as 'the village' and in those days it certainly looked like a village. The house looked fine with a reasonably sized back garden and was surrounded by open land, mostly fields and farmland. I had come off the Garnet for one voyage to move in but Rita already had most of the place ready. So it was a leave spent looking around the area.

Then I was sent for by Kingstons and informed that I was being transferred to the Kingston Emerald. The Emerald was like the Jacinth and had done only one voyage. It was one of the new ships but there was a difference concerning our next voyage. Kingston Emerald, along with Kingston Turquoise and the two from Hamlings, the St Celestin and the St Leger, were going on a new expedition, 'salting'.

This was a new process, where the cod was split and salted instead of being frozen. There was only one problem, our fishermen were not acquainted with splitting, so we would have to take on an extra fourteen men who were experienced splitters. These men were Faroe fishermen and the Emerald's focsle was converted quickly into new quarters to house them.

So we got ready. Salt was shipped from Cuxhaven in Germany and put on board along with a huge quantity of stores, fuel and water.

We were informed that it would be a six-week voyage and in March 1954, off we sailed.

Our first port of call was Thurshaven in the Faroe Islands, where we picked up the fourteen new crewmen, the 'splitters'.

We then set sail for Greenland. The four ships

Robert Baillie

Kingston Turquoise

were the Kingston Emerald with skipper Sid Duffield and me as radio officer. The Kingston Turquoise with skipper, Bill Cornish and radio officer, Stansfield. The St Celestin with skipper Bert Robbie and radio officer Len Conman. And the St Leger, with skipper Percy May and radio officer Doug Craig.

The ship was very heavy so our voyage to Cape Farewell was at a very moderate speed and took us longer than normal.We passed Cape Farewell at a safe distance and proceeded on a course for Cape Desolation, then up to the fishing banks with names like No Name Bank, Frederikshab Bank, Danas and Fyllas. As we passed Desolation the wind started to increase. Godthab Radio had given out a gale warning earlier and as the four ships proceeded up the Davis Straits the weather had already deteriorated. The wind had increased from the northeast and the temperature had dropped below zero. Soon a northeast storm had sprung up and we quickly started to ice up as the temperature dropped further. We already had a serious situation to deal with. We had to try to get some of the ice off but as we could only dodge head to wind, the huge seas across our bows were icing the ship up further. Steadily the masts, riggings, wires and the ship's rails and decks were icing up severely.

For twenty-four hours we ran afore the wind, with all the crew including the fourteen Faroe crewmen chopping ice continuously.

After three days like this the ice was winning and we were now in a critical condition, top heavy with ice and threatening to topple over. We had to do something quickly.

We called Godthab Radio, Godthab being the capital of Greenland - now also known as Nuuk - to speak to the Governor and ask permission to enter the port. As soon as he heard about the conditions we were

Robert Baillie

suffering and our dilemma we were granted permission to enter Godthab.

Our charts were not very good for entering Godthab and St Celestin's radar had broken down but we had to get in or perish. Kingston Emerald led with St Celestin astern, then Turquoise and St Leger. We navigated the rocks and entered the sound to Godthab. A small fishing vessel came out and seamen came on board to guide us into Godthab. We entered the port and went alongside, St Celestin first, as he had to get the radar repaired, followed by Emerald, Turquoise and Leger.

What a sight we were. You could hardly recognise us as ships, we just looked like blocks of ice. The Eskimos came down to help de-ice us whilst a number of Danish personnel with hot-water hoses set about clearing the ships. It was going to take a long time but at least we were safe.

So after a good night's sleep we woke up in Godthab. The normal fishing port was Faeringehavn but it was iced up and usually shut down at this time of year. It would not be open until the end of April, hence the reason that we had to come into Godthab.

While in port we were informed by the foreman of the Faroe splitters that we could not salt fish whilst it was freezing. So with the dreadful weather that we were experiencing, it looked as though we were going to be in Godthab for some time.

Later that morning one of the Faroe splitters told me that he had a sister in Godthab who seemingly had a problem with her radiogram and he wondered if I could look at it. At the time most of the port's technical engineers were away at home in Denmark and wouldn't return until April, so I made my way to the lady's house to see if I could help her. The fault on her radiogram was soon cleared for which she was most grateful.

WAITING FOR THE TIDE

In Godthab there were also a number of Danish nurses living in little chalets and when they heard that I was able to service their radios etc., I got myself a nice little job going round to their chalets and servicing what radio problems they had.

Whilst in Godthab, I also spent some time studying the Eskimo population. One of the interesting things was seeing some of the Eskimo girls in dresses that were made up of tiny beads. There must have been thousands of coloured beads threaded together.

Another occupation that I tried my hand at whilst in port was as a disc jockey.

The local radio station in Godthab didn't play much music for its listeners but I saw an easy way to provide a little more to keep them entertained.

We had an automatic record player on board the Emerald that played six or seven singles, one after the other. And after finding a suitable frequency that we could transmit on and that the locals could receive, I set up the record player and connected it through the transmitter. We were then able to play pop records for an hour or two each evening. I must add that this was definitely my first - and last - experience of being a DJ...

At the start of April the weather had improved greatly, so we could now leave port and head back to the fishing banks. We had one problem however; we were very short of food and fresh water. We could get neither in Godthab as they themselves waited for transport vessels to arrive with fresh supplies.

It was suggested that a trawler could come from Hull with the required supplies and we would meet it in Faeringehavn just down the coast.

We now moved out onto the banks and commenced fishing. On board our vessel the Faroe men had set up their splitting tables on the port side. Our

Top and left:
Faroe Islanders fish
'splitting' on board the
Kingston Emerald in 1955

Bottom:
Ashore in Godthab,
Greenland in 1955 with
ship's mate, A. Blanchard
and a group of Eskimo
children

crew gutted the fish, washed it and passed it to the Faroe men to split. The fish was put into the fishroom on salt and later turned and salted again.

We fished for many days and the fishing was quite heavy. We then got news that the Hull trawler was in the Davis Strait making for Faeringehavn. We stopped fishing and went into port to meet it and take on our stores. After getting our supplies, fuel and water we made our way out again. We fished up to the end of May and when we had enough tonnage we departed for Hull.

On our voyage home we were instructed to take our voyage to Esjberg in Denmark from where it would be shipped abroad.

When we arrived in Esjberg, it was June and very hot. We had already dropped the splitters in the Faroes, so now we just had to land the voyage. We were docked at a quay where the railway lines ran right alongside. Here our fish was unloaded into wagons then transported to its destination.

That first night, all the crewmen were given a sub in Kronas, the Danish currency. It was then all hands ashore for the night.

When our voyage had been landed we were instructed to proceed to Cuxhaven in Germany to pick up another cargo of salt, ready for our next voyage. We sailed to Cuxhaven, took on board the salt and then made our way home. When I arrived back in Cambridge Road, Hessle I had been away for twelve weeks. I remember that I was very glad to see my family and my home again after the harrowing experiences I had endured.

Sadly, this happy time ashore didn't last long however. A short time later skipper Sid Duffield and I left Kingston Emerald and I was informed that I would be going in the Kingston Sapphire with skipper, Charlie Hogg. The Sapphire was another new type of ship like

Robert Baillie

the Emerald but ironically, Charlie was 'Greenland mad' and spent many of his voyages round Cape Farewell.

So for the next year I was destined to be back in the area where I had just spent three months during one of the most dreadful winters I had ever experienced. An ordeal that ended with the terrible month of March, frozen up in the Davis Strait...

The progress in technology continued to move forward at a steady rate in the fishing industry. Trawlers were being fitted with the most up to date and more sophisticated electronic devices. The modern echo sounders could now record fish echoes. And radars with longer ranges, such as Loran, meant that transmitters that earlier had only medium wave facilities, were now operating on high frequencies, enabling us to communicate direct to Britain from any fishing ground.

With all this innovation, the role of the radio operator changed from one of 'sending and receiving messages' to that of an 'electronic officer'. These modern devices obviously required maintaining so we had to study this subject.

I sailed with skipper Charlie Hogg in Sapphire for over two years. Charlie of course was well known primarily as a 'Greenland skipper'. He was one of the few skippers who I sailed with who continuously navigated by sextant positions whilst crossing the North Atlantic.

When in Greenland Charlie fished continuously from the Kitsigut Islands to Cape Farewell and round Farewell to Walkendorff. The latter name usually sent a shudder through the trawler crews as it was regarded as one of the roughest grounds in the world. You had to be a good mender of nets there.

He fished there from late Spring to Summer as the

pack ice had disappeared and you had the fine, clear weather with just a few icebergs. During the winter Charlie mostly fished Bear Island and the Norwegian coast.

While I was sailing in Sapphire for over two years, another skipper, Cyril Burt took the vessel for a while. Cyril was an expert White Sea fisherman and during my sailing time with him we fished the White Sea, Kildin area. Kildin was the northerly Russian Naval Base for warships and submarines situated in the Kola Inlet. I knew this position very well from my Fleet-Air Arm days as a Telegraphist-Air Gunner on the aircraft carrier HMS Trumpeter, which was part of the convoy taking munitions, fuel etc to the Russians in their fight against the Germans. Kola Inlet was where we anchored, the convoy carrying on to Murmansk.

In 1958 I left Kingston Sapphire and joined Kingston Onyx with skipper Percy Bell. When I left Jacinth some four years earlier, I had parted company with John Neilsen. But here our paths crossed again, as he was the bosun on the Onyx.

Around this time relations between the Soviet Union and the west were at a low and because of this I often wondered if a World War III was more than a distinct possibility.

Percy Bell was another skipper who liked to fish most positions in the White Sea.

On arrival back from one trip there our office secretary informed me that two gentlemen from London wished to see me next door. I entered the room and was met by the two gents. One introduced himself as Commander Brookes. He and his colleague were from Naval Intelligence. He invited me to sit down and then explained why they had asked to meet me.

Commander Brookes had my record from my Fleet Air Arm service and various other details. He even

THE SPYMASTER - OFFICIAL

Christmas card reveals secret

By Hannah Start and Jonathan Davis

NEWS REPORTERS

DRAMATIC new evidence today reveals Commander John Brookes, who was based on the city fish dock throughout the 1960s, WAS a Government agent.

The Government still refuses to even discuss the enigmatic figure said to be the Cold War spymaster who directed a top secret spying operation on the Soviet fleet using city trawlermen.

But the Mail has now acquired a Christmas greeting card sent and signed by Commander Brookes dated 1965 bearing the Ministry of Defence name and crest.

It is the first time his name has officially been linked to the Government department.

Ex-skippers claim Commander Brookes used trawlermen as his eyes and ears in the Arctic fishing grounds close to important Soviet submarine bases.

He is said to have armed more than 50 skippers with cameras and radio equip-

have for and I was told it was nothing to do with him," persisted and my father called the whole family into the living room and told us of his work.

Mr Scott senior revealed the man Commander Brookes provided cameras and radio equipment to monitor Soviet shipping. The equipment was taken away before he died in 1976.

In 1969 Gavin saw at first hand his father take pictures of a passing Soviet ship while sailing with him in the White Sea.

Other skippers claim they met the Commander in the old White Fish Authority building on the top floor office of Tower CEA (Ship Supply).

Mr Terry Tarrah, now 52, who sailed with city trawler firm Boyd Line said: "He was a well known figure on the docks. He often used to come into our office and check which ships were due back and which were about the head off.

An MoD spokesman wouldn't comment on the role of Commander Brookes but admitted a limited number of fishing vessels assisted the government. He said it was normal for trawlermen to provide information they discovered in day-to-day activities.

THE GAUL: TIME FOR THE TRUTH

Some relatives of the Gaul's crew believe she may have been on a spying mission at the time of her disappearance in 1974.

The Christmas card was sent to Frank Scott, a radio operator on trawlers, who has since died.

His son Gavin Scott (48), from Withernsea, kept it as a teenager. Another letter from Brookes asks a skipper to drop off film at his dock-side office.

The MoD card also bears the signature of a Michael Kyle Pope, adding another mysterious figure to the city spy network.

Mr Scott broke his 30-year-silence to reveal how he first discovered his father's secret work.

He said: "When I was about 14 or 15 years old, I came home and someone was talking to my dad. I heard my father talk-

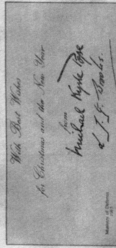

VITAL CLUE: The signature of Commander John Brookes (right) on this Christmas Card (above) is the first official time his name and the Government department.

With Best Wishes
for Christmas and the New Year
from
Michael Kyle Pope
& J.F. Bowles.

Ministry of Defence 1965

knew that I was married and had one daughter.

He then spoke about Britain's relations with the Soviet Union and explained that information regarding the movement of Soviet warships and submarines was of vital importance to the west. He next pointed out that British trawlers had access to the Barents Sea and the White Sea. And he asked me if I would participate in observing the movements and gaining information about the Soviet Fleet around Kildin and Kola Inlet and pass it on to Naval Intelligence.

May I point out this was strictly voluntary. It was up to me whether I agreed to do it or not.

I was a bit amused at all this since a few years before I had been assisting the Russians during World War II when they were on our side.

I told Commander Brookes that I would take part and asked him what my duties entailed.

He informed me, 'You will be given some sophisticated equipment including a long range camera, a long range telescope and a book containing silhouettes of all known Soviet warships and submarines.'

Also included was a pair of binoculars but Commander Brookes explained that although they looked like ordinary binoculars, they were fake ones and actually contained a radio receiver.

This meant that when I looked at a ship through them I was able to tune into the ship's radar and pick up a signal that was transferred to a small tape recorder situated out of sight on the bridge.

So with all this information I said goodbye to my two visitors and left the room.

Once outside the office I thought to myself, Good gracious - I'm a spy!

Top: Kingston Onyx   Bottom: Sailing through the Norwegian fiord

CHAPTER 6
ANDALUSITE & BERYL

We sailed again in the Kingston Onyx bound for the White Sea and Russia. This time however I was sailing in a different capacity because as well as working for the fishing fleet I was also working for Naval Intelligence. My job was to observe and log the movements of the Northern Soviet Navy based in Kildin and the Kola Inlet.

I had been given a brown leather case containing all my devices for use in observing Russian warships and submarines. I should point out here that it was well known that Russian trawlers were also engaged in spying while fishing around our coasts.

We made our usual course to the north Norwegian fiords and on leaving Honningsvag made our way to the White Sea. Now as well as Kildin being the North Russian Naval base, outside the 'Kildin' limit line there was some very good fishing to be had so British trawlers were seen frequently fishing in the area.

Kildin was an extra line on the chart that the Russians had made themselves, indicating no fishing vessel to fish inside this line. This on the chart was the Soviet Navy's training ground so if you wanted to observe their navy on their manoeuvres, the long-range telescope was the answer. We carried one for the next year or so while fishing Kildin. With the aid of my telescope I observed and logged movements of warships and submarines, checking their numbers and silhouettes with my 'special book' of Soviet warships.

A funny incident happened during this adventure. My wife Rita was totally unaware that I was taking part in this work. But while I was away on one voyage she was sorting out one of my drawers in our bedroom and stumbled on a bag containing books and silhouettes of Soviet warships, which were spares that I had left at home.

She got in a bit of a panic over this unexpected discovery and more so when one evening, just before I was due to dock, there was a tap at the front door. It was a gentleman dressed immaculately in a blue suit, a blue Burberry and a trilby, who inquired if I had arrived home yet. She informed him that I hadn't but I was due soon and asked if he would like to leave a message.

'No, that's all right thank you,' the gentleman replied and left without any further explanation.

The gentleman in question was Commander Brookes, who was apparently in temporary residence in Hessle, not far from Cambridge Road. He seemingly was on route to London that evening and as I was docking that same evening had called for a briefing on the voyage that I had just completed.

I sailed with Percy Bell for a long period in Onyx. Another ship had joined Kingstons from Marr's called the Farnella and later was renamed the Kingston Andalusite. Now although the Andalusite was a single bridge compared to the Onyx's three, it was much faster. This was a great advantage, being quicker to the fishing grounds and you could remain there longer on the grounds and catch the same tide as the slower ship that had to leave earlier.

So Percy and I changed ships to the Andalusite. I still maintained my observing work but during this period Gary Powers, an American pilot was shot down in a U2 spy plane, captured and paraded in public as a United States spy. Things also moved forward in the space race, with Russia putting the first man into orbit around the Earth and later the Americans landing a man on the moon. And in the pipeline were satellites that could orbit the Earth photographing everything in sight.

WAITING FOR THE TIDE

The reason that I mention all this was that our little mission was scaling down gradually. But still I was proud to have taken part, doing what I thought was my duty in those sinister days of the Cold War…

The Kingston Andalusite was a single bridge vessel. There was a bunk in the radio room and down below was a cabin next to skipper Percy Bell's, seemingly for the navigator. But Percy said this would be my cabin whilst sailing on this ship. It was very comfortable.

One alarming incident on Andalusite happened when we were sailing to the White Sea. As we approached Svino one of our engine cylinder heads blew and we had to limp to Harstad for repair. Docking in Harstad, we had to 'blow down', that means getting rid of your steam and power.

During the night a terrific storm blew up and we were parted from our mooring ropes and were soon drifting helplessly. We had no power but far more serious than that, we were drifting astern towards the gates of the dry dock that contained a Norwegian warship with all its crew on board.

The alarm was raised and the Norwegian crew were evacuated from their vessel. Slowly we edged astern towards the gates. It was a very serious situation. If we had hit the dock gates and forced them open, we would have fallen into the dry dock on top of the Norwegian vessel.

Then suddenly, a Norwegian ocean-going tug leaving Harstad for Bergen and hearing of our plight came to our rescue. It got a line on us and held us up, before towing us to safety. We re-docked, completed our repair and carried on to the White Sea, returning later with a full ship.

Another episode that I remember whilst on the

Robert Baillie

Andalusite took place as we were bound for Greenland with skipper Arthur Moss, Percy Bell having the voyage off.

We were a day away from Cape Farewell when a similar fault occurred and another cylinder head blew. There was no port in Greenland that we could go to so we made our way to Reykjavik in Iceland. We limped slowly across the Denmark Strait and eventually arrived at our destination.

When we docked in Reykjavik we couldn't get any engineers ashore to help but luckily a British gunboat was also in port and their engineers came on board to give us assistance and the fault was cleared. We then abandoned our plan to go to Greenland and fished off Iceland where we got a good voyage.

The final incident on the Andalusite happened when we again set sail for the White Sea in late November. We arrived in the White Sea and fished on Skolpen Bank for the full voyage but we had a continuous northeast wind, which was icing the vessel, only slightly at first. The fishing was good and soon we were full up. We started to steam to Honningsvag to pick up a pilot but with heavy seas, strong winds and below zero temperatures we were soon heavily iced up. Our radar had ceased working so we proceeded into the Tana Fiord for shelter. The fault with our radar was in the scanner. I had to get up on the bridge to fix it. The crew rigged a tarpaulin over the scanner on top of the bridge and a wander lead with a light. It was freezing heavily up there and my fingers were soon numb with the severe cold. I cleared the fault, cleared the ice away from the scanner and returned to the bridge. We then proceeded to Honningsvag but when the pilot came out he wouldn't take us through until we got rid of the heavy ice on board.

All the crew got working with axes and hot water

hoses and eventually the pilot took us through. But on reaching Lodingen a full storm was blowing outside. With the ship being 'heavy' with fish it looked dangerous going outside. We then got permission to take another pilot to proceed through the south fiords, emerging into the North Sea south of Svino. We dropped our pilot and proceeded across the North Sea to Hull where we grossed £10,000.

I stayed ashore for Christmas and the New Year and after the break I was sent for to join the Kingston Beryl with skipper Bill Hornby. The Beryl had just joined Kingstons but there was a difference, she was a motor ship not like the old, steam-powered vessels.

The other fascinating thing was that the Beryl was the first, variable pitch propeller trawler out of Hull. The difference between her and the older vessels, was that you moved the older ships by increasing the engine speed, which turned the propeller faster according to whether you wanted slow, half or full speed. And to stop you simply stopped the engines. But with Beryl, with her variable pitch propeller, the engine stayed at the one speed all the time and you moved the ship, slow, half or full speed by varying the pitch of the propeller with a special handle and dial on the bridge. To stop the ship, the blades were simply put to neutral.

The Beryl was a single bridge ship with accommodation running from the bridge to midships port side, which included the officers' mess, crews mess, galley, chief engineer, 2nd engineer, Radio officer and third engineer's mess. And with a modern radio room and the Captain's quarters on the bridge, it was quite a modern little ship.

Skipper Bill Hornby was a true gentleman and a man who always put the safety of the crew first. He would never fish in bad weather but was always in the top earners. I sailed with Bill for a while, then he left

Top: Bill Hornby on Kingston Beryl   Bottom: The Engine Room

WAITING FOR THE TIDE

Beryl and a new skipper, Ted Rimmer, took over for a period, followed by Ronnie Bunce.

During Ron's period as skipper, we were the first trawler to take a television set to sea. I had an old black and white set at home that had become obsolete, so I decided to try it out at sea.

I mentioned this to an ex-radio operator who was running a TV aerial company and he fitted me an aerial on the bridge and off we went. The only TV transmitter was Holme Moss, so we got a picture up to Flamborough but that was it.

After Ronnie Bunce left we fished on under our new skipper, Arthur Fulston. During this period we heard the news that Kingstons was going to be taken over by Hellyers. I decided to look for another private firm and thought that J. Marr seemed like a sophisticated firm with a number of fine ships and skippers of a very high standard.

It was then that I decided to join a marine radio company and choose Redifon. I was accepted and so began a new career at Marr's.

One of their vessels fitted by Redifon and requiring a radio officer was the Benella, commanded by Charlie O'Neill. I met him in Hessle and told him that I was moving from Kingstons and became his radio operator and sailed with him on his next voyage.

I was then introduced to Marr's and prepared for my first voyage. The Benella was a fine looking vessel with a good radio room and I had my own cabin.

Charlie always had a name as a 'stormy petrel', fishing in some rude weather, so off we sailed to Iceland and it certainly was a rough passage to the fishing grounds.

One thing I noticed at Marr's was that the food was superior and there was plenty of it. There also seemed to be plenty of radio and radar spares, in fact the

Top: Kingston Beryl   Bottom: Preparing the nets on Kingston Bery

Gutting fish on Kingston Beryl - 1950s

ship seemed generally well stocked with everything.

We arrived off southeast Iceland and commenced fishing. It was here that I learned about skipper O'Neill's technique of judging the markets. He seemed to arrive at every market with only a few other ships and therefore always got a very good price for his fish. So naturally, one of my jobs when we had nearly completed a voyage, was to gain information from Bear Island and the White Sea concerning which ships were leaving for market and what day they would arrive back in Hull to sell their voyage.

Now the Benella was quite a fast ship and whereas it usually took four to five days to steam back to Hull, it took us only 40 hours! So we could then get all the information, observe which was a slack day where maybe only two or three trawlers were landing and ensure we arrived at market on that day. It was bound to be a sure success.

I sailed with Charlie O'Neill for nearly three years fishing mostly around Iceland.

It was on one of these voyages that 'Surtsey' appeared. One minute there was clear sea, the next minute a volcanic island had appeared out of the water.

The first eruption was sighted early in the morning of November 14, 1963 about 18 km southwest of Heimaey, the largest of the Westman Islands. The eruptions lasted for nearly three and a half years before finally ceasing in June 1967.

Charlie had a voyage off so Peter Taylor took us to Greenland. It was his first trip as skipper and we caught a fine voyage. But on my return, I was informed that I was being brought off the Benella to sail in the Westella with one of Hull's greatest skippers, a fellow Scotsman named Bill Dreevers. Bill's name was legendary as a fisherman in Hull so it was with great pride that I sailed as radio officer with this famous and renowned seafarer.

One memorable voyage we sailed on Westella was to west Iceland. Bill was known as a great Iceland fisherman but on this voyage however the fishing was extremely slack on the west side, so we decided to steam to the east side.

It was then that I was surprised to hear my call sign in Morse. I was being called by another trawler and was simply given a course to steer with a brief message, 'Plenty of fish here'. But the course was going to bring us to east Greenland.

Bill Dreevers said that under the circumstances we would take a chance. We steamed on the course and at the same time listened on the same frequency, then listened on 410Khzs. This was a D/F frequency and as we stood by our direction finder, there he was sending out more messages in Morse. We took a bearing and yes, we were going in the right direction and eventually we sighted him. We were off Angmagssalik in East Greenland. Now it was essential that we keep our position on this small bank. This is where Loran came in. Day and night I took the Loran position and we ended up with a marvellous voyage of cod.

We came home to market and the next day when I read the Hull Daily Mail, there it was, the name - 'Bill Dreevers'. And we had made £15,000!

Bill Dreevers was also a masterful White Sea fisherman and Westella was certainly a ship that really made money. It was a great experience sailing with the maestro but later Bill decided to come ashore. One or two skippers commanded Westella later, the last one being Jack Fewster who was also a superb White Sea fisherman.

During my sailing days we were experimenting with depth sounders and what they termed 'narrow beam echo sounding'. Originally the beam was a wide

Robert Baillie

one so when you picked up a fish echo you weren't sure whether it was to port, starboard or directly under the keel.

On one voyage with Jack to the White Sea we had just left the Norwegian border and entered Russian waters when a Russian destroyer-type, naval vessel came alongside us and for the full voyage, day and night, he kept watch. Why? We never found out. He followed us to the Norwegian border when we were bound for home then left us. It was very strange. Had he picked up our experimental echo sounding trials?

Picking up fish echos was now a primary objective in echo sounding technique. Originally when you dropped your trawl on the fishing bank, was there fish any there? Imagine an echo sounding machine that could tell you before you dropped the trawl that there was definitely fish there. This was now the case. Sophisticated echo sounders and fish finders were now available that could pinpoint fish shoals very accurately.

Also gyro steering compasses were being installed. In this compass the axis of a freely spinning wheel was forced by electricity to point in the direction of the geographical pole. Once this has been achieved the gyro maintained itself in this position and was extremely accurate. At this stage of my fishing career, this innovation appeared to be the 'steering of the future'.

The future was also about to change in another way. The stern trawler factory ship, had been introduced with Marr's a leading pioneer with the MV Junella. These ships trawled from astern, the fish being hauled up a ramp and then down into a factory. This meant that there would be no more crews gutting on deck.

As I come to the end of my side trawling days, I must pay tribute to all those fishermen who worked under horrendous, freezing and stormy weather, for long hours on open decks. It was a high price to pay in order to get fresh cod and haddock to the table.

When we returned from our last voyage on Westella, Jack Fewster and I were informed that we were being transferred to the freezer factory vessel, Northella. The ship had just been completely rebuilt following an horrendous accident. Departing from Hull bound for Newfoundland she collided with the jetty at Killingholme and sustained severe damage. But now Northella was ready to sail again.

I boarded the vessel and was amazed by the size of the ship. There was a huge bridge with two radars, two echo sounders, Loran navigator, Decca navigator, gyro compass, automatic steering, a Decca plotter, a full radio room, two transmitters, three receivers, gyro controlled direction finder and a full amplifier section to speakers all over the ship.

There was also a spacious galley and a large factory where the fish was gutted and made into frozen blocks and then stored in a refrigerated fish room. Plus an Officers mess room, toilets, baths and bathroom on the second deck. A galley and crews' messroom on the lower deck. And outside a huge winch and trawl deck leading to the ramp astern.

Northella was powered by a diesel electric motor, housed in a massive engine room. And situated on the second deck was the gyro room and gyroscope. So here was all the electronic equipment which I would have to maintain. I realised that it was going to call for some serious studying to cope with it all.

Sailing day arrived and we were soon bound to Newfoundland where our voyage could be anything from seven to eight weeks, or even longer. Our normal track was to the Spurn LV, Flamborough, then to Pentland Firth, Cape Wrath, Butt Of Lewis, then across the North Atlantic to the Newfoundland fishing banks.

Robert Baillie

Navigating was mainly by Loran positioning while crossing the Atlantic, then by Decca Navigator closer to Newfoundland.

We had just passed Rockall when the Chief Engineer, my good friend Jimmy Powdrell, reported an electrical fault. Some of the wiring was the wrong gauge and had resulted in overheating. We had to make for Newfoundland for repairs.

After a few days we arrived in St Johns. It was summer and it was hot, over 80°. As soon as we docked, a team of shore electricians came on board and we were informed that it would take a few days to rewire the ship. So we then had an opportunity to take a good look around St Johns.

The operation of the freezer trawler fleet working as a group was different to the side fishing operation. In the side fishing operation, competition was great as you were dependent on the fresh fish market and your earnings were dependent on what your catch made on landing. So skippers were inclined to keep quiet about where they were fishing if they were alone and fishing was good.

The freezer trawler was different, they left Hull and stayed away until they were full up, as all fish caught was frozen into blocks and earnings were gauged on how many tons they landed. This was the reason that all freezer trawler skippers worked as a group exchanging information about the positions and the amount of fish caught. This is also where the radio officer became the main man in the group. We had what was called a 'schedule' that took place at 11am, 4pm and 11pm.

One freezer ship would take control and would be in control for one week before another took charge. The duty of the control ship was to call in on a certain radio frequency at the above times to every other freezer trawler in the group. The freezer would pass his information, made up of the position, what he was catching and at 23.00 hours, the total amount of fish that he had caught for the day.

All the information was sent in Morse code at all times. When the information was received, the radio officer would decode the messages and enter them into a schedule book before passing it to the skipper. This was a huge benefit to freezer trawler skippers because as they left Hull, they could obtain up to the minute information about the best fishing positions that were available and then make up their minds where to go.

St Johns had only one main street where all its shops and bars were situated. Any old freezer men will remember it well, and also our agent there Mr Humphries. He didn't dash on board for a dram but for a big mug of English tea with plenty of sugar.

After a week we were ready for sea. We received information from our group that hardly anyone was fishing around Newfoundland, most of them were off Greenland.

We left St Johns with a few of the crew nursing sore heads after sampling some shore rum called 'Screech'. It was aptly named, especially the following morning. We dropped our pilot and set course for Greenland where most of the group were. On approaching Greenland we heard reports that fishing had slackened off and the fish was in 'rough ground'.

Jack Fewster wasn't very happy at Greenland and after a day or two decided to go back to Newfoundland. We steamed back to a position called 'Flemish Gap', an isolated bank off the Grand Banks. When we arrived, there wasn't a single fishing vessel in sight and very few fish echoes. It looked bleak but as we searched around

Robert Baillie

we picked a group of ships on our radar and closing up to them we observed massive fish echos on our sounders. The ships were all Russian and they seemed very busy on their decks.

We shot our trawl and towed along but when we hauled we had burst our net with fish.

We had towed for too long. But after mending the net we shot and towed for a shorter period of time and soon had a full net. For the entire voyage we remained on this position keeping our position by Loran and Decca navigator.

The difference with the crew on this ship was that they worked below in the factory, gutting the fish, and putting them into freezers where they were formed into blocks and then stored in a frozen fish room. But the crew also had to be up on the open deck to pay the trawl away, haul it in or to mend the nets when necessary.

This was a stern trawler, the trawl being payed away down a ramp and out astern. The huge trawl winch was mostly under cover paying the wire warps away with the trawl. Eventually we were full up and set course for home.

When we arrived in dock after two months at sea, we landed our voyage at the special freezer quay on St Andrew's Dock. We had a full ship of 12,000 blocks of frozen fish, just over 500 tons. The crews were paid on a sliding scale of how many tons they landed, plus cod liver oil money.

We would be about seven days in dock but my work didn't stop, I had plenty to do before the start of our next voyage. My first job was to get all the radio, echo sounders, radars, gyro, Decca Navigator and Loran checked and if any spares were required, to order them ready for the next voyage. I then had to check any new equipment that had been put on board. As you can imagine operating and maintaining all this equipment

WAITING FOR THE TIDE

for a full voyage was no mean operation.

Once everything had been checked, it was leisure time at home for seven days. I think my wife had thought that we had got lost. Normally it was a three-week's voyage but this one lasted for two months.

We must give great credit to the fishermen's wives. These women had to not only be mother and father to their kids, but also had to take care of all the household chores and repairs, and of course pay the numerous bills during the long periods when their men were away...

Bottom: Rita, Patricia and me on Scarborough beach

CHAPTER 7
DEAR DIARY

In December 1967 we sailed for Greenland but when we arrived there was too much ice so we steamed to Labrador. This is where my diary starts on New Year's Day 1968.

I kept a diary every day of my life and in my stern trawling days, this diary contained all the fishing positions in latitude and longitude and the daily events that happened during the voyages. The following chapter shows how I recorded this information...

1968

Monday, January 1
We were fishing off Labrador, there was plenty of fish here.

Saturday, January 13
We were bound back to Hull.

Saturday, January 20
We docked at St Andrew's dock at 21.00 hours and landed 486 tons.

Monday, January 29
16.30 - Bound Newfoundland, Skipper Arthur Ness

Tuesday, January 30
Sailing through Pentland Firth.

Wednesday, January 31
Passed Rockall.

Thursday, February 1 – Sunday, February 4
North Atlantic, westerly gale all the way.

Monday, February 5
16.00 - Commenced fishing Newfoundland, position
52.30N 52.25W - we have come up to
very thick pack ice.

Tuesday, February 6
Laid all night, heavy pack ice.

09.00 dodging slowly eastwards through pack ice to a bit of clear water to fish.

Wednesday, February 7

Position 53.05N 53.40W - Laid all night in pack ice and clearing fish.

Thursday, February 8

Position 52.47N 52.40W - Pack ice but good fishing.

Friday, February 9

Good fishing but plenty of pack ice.

Saturday, February 10

SE strong winds, heavy pack ice, good fishing in clear pools.

Sunday, February 11

Position 52.48N 52.40W – Good fishing in 138 to 170 fathoms.

Monday, February 12

Position 52.48N 52.45W – Good fishing, 200 tons on board.

Tuesday, February 13

Steamed north to position 53.55N 52.52W. Good fishing in 200 fathoms. First haul 500 baskets.

Wednesday February 14 & Thursday February 15

Position 54N 53W - Good fishing.

Friday, February 16

01.00 - Stern trawler Ross Vanguard calls for assistance. His propeller has been fouled. He cannot move and is in pack ice.

01.10 – We answer the call. I take a direction finding bearing of him and proceed to his assistance.

03.00 – Find Vanguard in pack ice, position 54.14N 53.00W.

04.00 – We fire four rockets with lines but they are fouled in ice.

05.00 – We attempt to swing round trying to get a bit of clear water, fire a rocket, Vanguard picks up line.

08.10 – Vanguard has got our wire on board and we

are now pulling him clear of the ice and commence towing him at 6 knots to St Johns, Newfoundland.

12.00 – Towing at 6 knots keeping clear of ice pack.

Saturday February 17

09.00 – Still towing Vanguard all day.

19.00 – Saturday night – towline parted, took us 7 hours to get ship back on tow.

Sunday February 18

09.00 – Still towing Vanguard.

21.00 – Sunday night – towline parts again, took 5 hours to get him back.

Monday February 19

09.00 – Still towing Vanguard at 5 knots.

17.00 – Passed island of Baccaleau, 38 miles to go.

Tuesday February 20

01.00– Off St Johns waiting for pilots.

03.15 – In St Johns with Vanguard safe.

22.00 – Left St Johns bound for Belle Isle, where we came from.

Wednesday February 21

Still steaming to Belle Isle.

Thursday February 22

Position 53N 52 W - Ran into pack ice again, SW force 10 wind, temperature –21°F.

We are now moving at a slow speed through this pack ice. The wind is gale force 10 with the temperature dropping still further.

Friday February 23

Position 52N 51W - Dodging northerly, now clear a bit from ice.

Position 53.50N 52.05W – We are in heavy pack ice again.

Saturday February 24

Position North of 52.00N. It seems Belle Isle/Labrador is covered in ice.

Now back at 52.42N 52.20W –Tried to get to 53.20N

but stuck in pack ice.

Sunday February 25
Position 52.42N 52.20W – Fishing in pack ice but very good fishing.
18.00 – We are getting out. Surrounded by heavy pack ice.

Monday February 26
Laid all night in pack ice 52,30N 51.00W – trying to get to 53.30N 52.28W.
19.15 – Pushing our way through heavy ice, now with crowd of Russian vessels. Position 53.00N 52.00W Plenty of pack ice around.

Tuesday February 27
Fishing in a clear pool surrounded by pack ice.

Wednesday February 28
Position 52.35N 52.05W. Still fishing but surrounded by pack ice, weather fine now, it is calm, the reason being we are deep in the ice field.

Thursday February 29
Position 52.40N 51.30W. Still fishing, very heavy ice pack.

Friday March 1
Nearly 500 tons on board. Still in heavy pack ice.

Saturday March 2
Wind is now SE force 8. No swell because surrounded by ice.

Sunday March 3
Tried to get to 53.30N but turned back, ice too heavy. We have now probably damaged the keel and side plates with ice.

Monday March 4
Fishing in heavy pack ice 52.20N 57.20W. Over 500 tons on board.

Tuesday March 5
08.30 – Full ship now. Proceeding home. We are surrounded by ice moving slowly through heavy ice

field. Course 075°T. For seven hours shoved our way through heavy ice and in position 52.30N 49.57W - we came out into open water, the first clear water seen for twelve days.

Wednesday March 6
01.00 – Now in the Atlantic.

Thursday March 7
Position 56.00N 26.00W North Atlantic – weather fine.

Saturday March 9
15.00 – Passed Rockall, weather - westerly 4.

Tuesday March 12
04.00 - Docked in Hull and landed 511 tons but had to go into King George dry dock as ice damage to the keel and plates was suspected.

It had been the worst voyage ever for pack ice. Every day inside the ice field there was a potential danger to both the men and the ship. Northella was the only British ship fishing in this position, the only other vessels were Russians. But here once again I witnessed the terrible conditions that the fishermen had to tolerate in order to catch fish.

Although the ship was a freezer and most of the work was done below deck in the factory, one has to remember that the crewmen were still out on the open deck while paying the trawl away, hauling and net mending. There was also still the force 10 winds and temperatures of -20°F to endure.

Having read the diary entries above you will have noticed the accurate latitude and longitude positions. The Loran navigator accomplished this. It was one of my duties to take the Loran positions, then transfer them to the fishing or navigation charts. This enabled us to navigate freely anywhere in the North Atlantic.

Robert Baillie

Tuesday March 19
20.30 – Sailed from King George Dock bound for Greenland.

Thursday March 21
Through Pentland Firth and into North Atlantic.

Sunday March 24
Midnight – arrived at Cape Farewell, laid all night due to threat of ice.

Monday March 25
08.00 – Set course for Cape Egede (CHECK SP)
14.30 – Off Cape Egede, pack ice sighted, slow speed, commenced fishing, first haul 250 baskets of good cod.

Tuesday March 26
Left Cape Egede, too much pack ice, now slow through pack ice, off Cape Desolation clear and steaming to No Name Bank, weather NNW 9.

Wednesday March 27
Fishing at No Name Bank off Frederikshab, West Greenland, isolated icebergs around.

Thursday March 28
Lot of foul work at No Name Bank - Position Umanak 090°T 30 miles off. (EDIT?)

Monday April 1
14.00 – We are now steaming to Labrador – too much ice at Greenland.

Tuesday April 2
Still steaming to Labrador.
21.00 – Pack ice, slow speed – altered course to 080°T in order to clear ice.

Wednesday April 3
Stopped all night during hours of darkness alongside heavy pack-ice field.
08.30 – Daylight - proceeding again along ice field.
21.00 – Arrived at German and Russian ships – all ships fishing in position 55.10N 54.50W.

WAITING FOR THE TIDE

Good fishing reported.
Thursday April 4
There are up to 300 baskets per haul in 190-220 fathoms, also good fishing 53.03N. 52.06W in 195-200 fathoms. But there is heavy ice in the area. Tried to get to 53.03N 52.06W but heavy pack ice stopped us. Returned to 55.00N 54.56W - stopped all night, when daylight comes will try again.
Saturday April 6
All yesterday shoved our way through pack ice, got clear.
22.45 - set course for 53.00N 52.10W.
15.00 - Returning North again as pack ice is all over, cannot get into any bank from 53°N to 56°N. The pack ice is as far North as Mugford, North Labrador.
Sunday April 7
Still steaming north, have passed miles of pack ice. We will soon be near Hudson Strait and Hudson Bay entrance.
Monday April 8
Pack ice too heavy to get into fish at 58°20N 59°25W
10.00 – We are now bound for Greenland again. The question is when or where do we get clear of ice?
Tuesday April 9
16.00 – Commenced fishing at No Name Bank, Greenland, 3 hauls total 1,300 baskets cod, position Umanak 040°T, 28.5 miles by radar, 65-90 fathoms, isolated icebergs, weather fine.
Wednesday April 10
Laid all night clearing fish, the fish goes to the bottom here.
16.00 – midnight - weather fresh northerly wind, one or two icebergs.
Thursday April 11
Same position, lot of fish here, 500 baskets for 1 hour tow. Mostly German ships here.

Robert Baillie

Friday April 12
Plenty of fish, same position 050° bearing 21-22 miles
– 90 fathoms.

Saturday April 13
Fishing Frederikshab Bank, up to 400 baskets here in
165 fathoms. German, French, Portuguese, Spanish
ships here and a few ships steaming here from
Newfoundland.

Sunday April 14
Same position but stopped during the night because of
very bad weather with heavy seas coming on deck.

Monday April 15
Winds decreased but fish has moved with the bad
weather.

Tuesday April 16
08.00 – We have a crewmember injured, with a
suspected broken leg. I call on the radio for any
hospital ship in the area. The German hospital ship
Posiedem answers my call and is coming to our ship.
10.00 – Posiedem arrives and a doctor comes on board
and the crewmember is transferred to the hospital ship.
We commence fishing again.

Saturday April 20
On information received from the Portuguese vessel
Santa Cristin, we move to Danas Bank. Good fishing
but very rough ground. Our nets are continuously torn.
Crews mending nets all day. Now steamed to Fyllas
Bank – weather now northwest 8. Moved slowly to
Banana Bank but did not shoot trawl. Now steaming
back to Frederikshab. Commenced fishing, average
70-120 baskets.

Friday April 26
06.00 – Bound home with 420 tons on board.

Saturday April 27
Had to pass 140 miles south of Cape Farewell to clear
ice – now in the Atlantic.

WAITING FOR THE TIDE

Thursday May 2
08.00 – We docked in Hull.

We were now in dock landing our voyage at the freezer berth, free from all pack ice and iceberg problems. It was May and the weather was fine and warm, what a contrast. Now I could enjoy my time at home and think about taking the family out.

My daughter Patricia was now fifteen years old but I had actually not seen her grow up because of continuously being at sea. So getting the car into action, it was time to take Rita and Patricia to some of the East Coast resorts. First we went to Bridlington. How strange it was looking out to sea and not seeing any icebergs. We spent a full day there. Then the following day our next destination was Flamingo Park Zoo.

The next few days were spent at home trying a bit of gardening. This was quite a novelty as it was usually the freezerman's wife who looked after the garden while he was away at sea.

But soon it was sailing time again. We sailed at 14.00 hours on Wednesday May 8, once again bound for Greenland and back to the Frederikshab Bank.

We commenced fishing at 04.00 on Tuesday May 14. The same icefields were still around but the fishing was very slack. So we steamed North to Fiskanes Bank, then to a position near Little Fiskanes Bank. Here we saw a number of Portuguese schooners. Their type of fishing was line fishing, done by individual Portuguese men in small boats called Dhorys. They were cast off from their schooners and line fished all day. At the end of the day they came back to their schooner and were lifted on board with their catch, which was then processed. These ships were at sea for months. We steamed back to Frederikshab and the fishing was good for the remainder of the voyage.

Robert Baillie

Tuesday June 4
08.00 - we left for home with a full ship of 12,316 blocks.

Wednesday June 5
15.30 abeam Cape Farewell 66 miles off to clear icefield now steaming in the North Atlantic – weather fine sunshine.

Tuesday June 11
Docked at St Andrews Dock and landed our voyage of 500 tons.

Saturday June 15
Sailed for Newfoundland again – very slack fishing so steamed to Greenland – no fish at Greenland.

Tuesday July 16
Steamed from Greenland to Iceland - fished at Iceland – very slack.

Wednesday July 24
Docked in Hull - my holidays were now due.

Since my last visit to Scotland my father had once again been promoted, on this occasion to Stationmaster at Crookston Station, Glasgow. So on Sunday August 4 all the family set off to Scotland to my parents' new house. A great welcome awaited us with plenty of tales to tell and of course a look around the new place.

It was beautiful warm weather. We travelled to Edinburgh and round Loch Lomond, The Trossachs and across to the east coast to Fife, visiting my brother in that area, then along the beaches of the east coast resorts to complete a great holiday.

We returned to Hull on Monday August 19. While on holiday it was my daughter's birthday, she was now sixteen. Doesn't time fly, I thought to myself.

Back home we did the full circuit of Bridlington, Scarborough, Whitby, the Moors and then to Knaresborough. September 8 was my birthday and we spent it visiting Blackpool to see the lights. I enjoyed a really wonderful time at home but all too soon the holiday was over.

I signed back on the Northella and on Friday September 20 we sailed for Newfoundland. We commenced fishing off Labrador, position 54.00N 54.00W and averaged 300-400 blocks. We remained around Labrador and Belle Isle where the fishing was good.

On Saturday October 26 after fishing for nearly a month, the winds began to increase and later rose to storm force. We had to stop fishing because of the bad weather. The weather decreased but so had the fish. We now steamed to Le Grand Nord Bank, Newfoundland.

We had one good day and landed 516 blocks, but easterly gales again increased to storm force. So on Tuesday October 31 position 48.40N 50.00W at 10.30am we left for home with about 400 tons.

In the Atlantic, it was easterly then southeast gales all the way, before we finally docked in Hull on Saturday November 9.

We were informed that we would be on a Lloyds Insurance Survey for approximately five weeks, so believe it or not I was going to be in dock until after Christmas.

I had never really had a long stay at home over Christmas before so this was going to be something new for me.

We were told that we would be sailing on Boxing Day so off I went to get the turkey, the Christmas tree, the wine and the presents.

How strange it was not being tossed around in a storm on Christmas Day. And what an enjoyable Christmas we had and how more special it seemed when during a lifetime at sea you had spent more Christmases away than at home.

Robert Baillie

We were then ordered to sail on Friday December 27 so when the shoremen were getting ready for New Year we were back at sea.

Friday, December 27
13:00 hours sailed bound for the Norwegian coast passed Svino and Skomvaer.

Tuesday December 31
We are now steaming along the north Norwegian coast making for North Cape, Norway.
New Year's Eve - we had a few beers and a dram but we were soon going to be on the fishing grounds.

Wednesday, January 1, 1969 - New Year's Day
Still steaming to the Norwegian coast.

Thursday, January 2
We arrived at North Cape and commenced fishing in position 72.00° N. 27.00° E. where very good fishing was reported all over. There is a lot of fish off the North Cape from this position to 72.30°N. 25°E.

Saturday, January 18
We are averaging 300 to 500 baskets a haul and fishing in 140-160 fathoms. At this rate of fishing we will have a full ship in a very short time.

A new role that I had taken on as radio officer was meteorology. My duty was to report in daily to the Metro Centre at Bracknell in England with details of the wind direction etc., the type of clouds, and barometer and temperature readings. We were supplied with all the necessary equipment.

I coded the messages and then sent them in Morse Code to Portishead Radio in the Bristol Channel. You could also send the messages to any coast station and you were given a priority with this message over any normal telegram dispatch.

WAITING FOR THE TIDE

Tuesday, January 28
We have now been fishing for 25 days and fishing has been very heavy. We are full up and bound back to Hull.

Saturday, February 1
18:00 hours - Docked in Hull, landed 527 tons of cod.

Wednesday, February 12
03:00 hours - Left St Andrew's Dock bound back to the Norwegian coast.

Thursday, February 13
20:00 hours - Passed Svino LH.

Friday, February 14
09.00 hours - Passed Halten Bank.

Saturday, February 15
Passed Andenes, now steaming to the north Norwegian coast, we are bound to fishing grounds off Hjelmsoy, North Norway.

Sunday, February 16
In position 71.05° N. 23.16° E. at 08.00 hours the Marr's trawler Thornella calls for assistance.
He has his net round his propeller and is drifting to shore. We are now proceeding to his assistance. We sight the Thornella.
09:00 - Preparing to fire a rocket with a line to him.
09.10 - Fired a rocket, Thornella picks up the line then drags wire abroad.
09.35 - Now towing Thornella to Hammerfest, North Norway. The weather - force 3.
17.30 - Entered Hammerfest with Thornella now berthed safely.
21.00 - We leave Hammerfest bound for the fishing grounds.

Tuesday, February 18
Fishing 10 miles off Fruholmen, averaging 70 to 100 baskets of fish, increasing in the evening, two hauls of 180 and 200 baskets.

Northella in pack-ice off Labrador, February 1968

WAITING FOR THE TIDE

Wednesday, February 19
Fish has gone inside limit line, we are steaming to North West Bank.

Thursday, February 20
Fishing North West Bank, very good fishing in 150 fathoms, then during the night in 70 fathoms.

Saturday and Sunday - Laid clearing fish, we are now going to fish Malangen Bank during the daytime and North West Bank during nighttime, good fishing.

Friday, February 28
Fish gone now, steaming to North Cape in Norway to a position where the Norwegians reported good fishing.

Sunday, March 2
Fishing but long tows of four hours duration. We are now steaming back to North Cape, then fished this area until Wednesday, March 12.

Thursday March 13
08:00 hours - bound for Hull with 10,750 blocks on board. On our homeward journey the winds have increased to southeast storm force 10

Tuesday, March 18
07:00 hours – docked in Hull and landed 489 tons for 34 days.

On Monday, March 24 at 09.30 we sailed for Newfoundland but this voyage was completely hampered by pack ice, plus we had to go into St John's for a repair to the boiler.

We attempted fishing from Grand Nord to Labrador but ice packs hindered our operations. Greenland was out of the question with all grounds covered by ice fields. So on Saturday, May 3 at 04.30 we left for home. It had not been a very good voyage and we landed only 330 tons.

CHAPTER 8
NORTHELLA

Pack ice wasn't the only danger waiting in the dark and freezing Arctic Ocean. Whilst fishing off Newfoundland, Labrador and Greenland I encountered countless tragic incidents that happened during these voyages.

On Christmas Eve 1966, we were fishing in a position south of Miquelon, Newfoundland when we heard the distress call from another stern trawler, Finbarr.

He was on fire!

At the same time as this was happening, we had a casualty on board. Our second engineer had fallen and broken his leg. We had to get him into port. The nearest to us was Sydney, Cape Breton Island, Nova Scotia. We called Sydney and asked permission to come in with the injured man and it was granted.

We docked on Christmas morning, went alongside the quay and put the man ashore. But we hit a snag. We should have carried our vaccination cards on board. This was a rule in Canada, you had to show the yellow card to prove that you had been vaccinated for smallpox. But they had not been put on board, so on Christmas Day we all had to go to the clinic in Sydney to be vaccinated.

After that we put to sea again into the most vicious storm we had experienced, a force 12.

We had to dodge head to wind with huge seas breaking over as it was far too rough to have Christmas dinner so we had to do without.

It was only the following day that we heard how the tragedy had ended and that the Finbarr had sunk. The next incident occurred while we were again fishing south of Newfoundland. The weather had changed rapidly and about midnight the wind had increased to full storm. We had got all our fishing gear on board and were dodging head to wind, when we heard a call from a small ship that was requiring immediate assistance.

I called the vessel for his position and found we could get to him within an hour or two. We brought our vessel round with the storm at its height and proceeded to him at a reduced speed. After a while we spotted the small ship's lights in the darkness but there was no way that we could get near him because of the high seas. The small ship was being tossed around like a cork. We managed to get fairly near to him but it seemed that his transmitter had gone.

I called him and said, 'Flash a light if you can hear me.'

A little light flashed and I then informed him that it was too dangerous to attempt taking anyone off but we would come up near him, put him on our lee side and attempt to shelter him until they could be rescued.

This we did. We came broadsides to wind and seas and sheltered him for 36 hours, every hour or so asking him to flash a light if he could still hear me.

Then, at about three in the morning out of the blue Northella received a call.

'This is the United States Coastguard ship Castle Rock, we can get to him and get the people off.'

He did so but shortly after taking them off, the little boat sunk.

We learned that the occupants of the vessel had been a family moving house by boat and later received a telegram from the Canadian Authorities thanking us for our great effort in saving the family.

Another episode that I will never forget was during our first venture of fishing in the Gulf of St Lawrence. The fishing was very slack in South

Robert Baillie

Newfoundland when we got information from a Canadian fisherman that there was plenty of cod in the Gulf. So we made our way through the Cabot Strait to a position off the Magdalen Islands, then fished our way past Anticosti Island to a position off Corner Brook and here was fisherman's paradise, with trawls full of cod after each haul.

As we were fishing however a Canadian gunboat came up to us. Their officer came on board and there seemed a bit of a discrepancy as to whether our licence covered us fishing there.

Fortunately we were already full up with cod so there was not much we could do about it. We were let off and immediately set off for home.

When we arrived in Hull we landed over 500 tons but we never returned to the area again...

I should comment here on the work that was done by the crew of Northella. When the fish was hauled on board it was dropped into the factory through a door at the top of the ramp in the deck and down into the fish space. The fish was then gutted, washed and put on an endless belt to arrive alongside the freezers. Finally, the fish was inserted into the freezers and after a certain time was taken out as a frozen block and sent by lift down into the frozen fish hold.

I have given some brief details of the crew's duties on board Northella but I would like to add a more precise description of each crewmember:

The Captain

He was in overall command of the vessel and during fishing the main fishing master, his hours of duty were more or less continuous.

The First Mate

Next in position to the captain. His duties

included overseeing all operations on deck, relieving the Captain of fishing duty whilst he had a period below. Part of the watch and in charge of it during steaming. His hours of duty – watchkeeping times shared with Second Mate and Third Mate.

The Second Mate

Mostly in charge of deck work and steaming with bridge watch hours of duty similar to the First Mate.

The Third Mate

Similar to Second Mate's hours of duty and watch hours.

Note: on Sidewinders the above positions were Skipper, Mate, Bo'sun and Third Hand but on the larger vessels it was Captain, First Mate, Second Mate and Third Mate.

The Chief Engineer

Here was a most important man on board the vessel, in charge of the engine room, refrigeration and anything that moved, such as winches, factory machinery etc.

Credit must go to these men, many of whom had come up from the old trawlers to take charge of these modern giants.

Hours of duty were watch hours but could be called out at any time if required.

2nd Engineer and 3rd Engineer

Back up to the Chief and made up the Engineering Department, duties were mainly oilmen, cleaners and general engine room duties.

The Cook and Second Cook.

Here was a very important pair. Here was not just a cook preparing meals but a baker, a butcher and a confectioner, all in one. His hours of duty were long, starting at 04.00 baking fresh bread and rolls, then daily preparing breakfast, dinner and tea, suppers were usually cold fare.

Robert Baillie

The Factory Manager

He was a crewman appointed to this job after training, his job was the production and storage of blocks of fish. One has to remember that a full ship was over 12,000 blocks, each approximately 112lbs.

The Radio Officer

Here I can only describe the duties that I undertook during an average day.

Called at 06.30am, a shower and shave every morning, breakfast at 7.30 and plenty of it.

8.00 Radio Room – take Loran positions, then make my way to the bridge to apply Loran position to chart and receive a position for transmission to Hull.

Note: Insurance Rules stated that all stern trawler's positions had to be sent daily at this time.

My next job was to take my barometer and thermometer readings, cloud formations etc.

Code this up and after coding our morning position, call by Morse Code, either Wick or Portishead Radio and despatch both messages, one, my daily position, the other, my weather observations. Next, listen out to Wick and Portishead traffic lists for incoming telegrams.

Proceed round the bridge and the gyro room to check that all units were working okay.

11:00 - Start round up of all stern trawler fishing information, all messages are in code. Decode them and present this information to the skipper.

12:30 – Dinner.

16.00 – Round up again of fishing information. Listen out again for traffic lists.

18.00 - Observations of the weather again.

18.30 - Teatime.

Throughout the day kept a continuous watch 500 kHz - distress frequency.

23.00 – Once again, round up of stern trawler

fishing information.

Midnight - Weather observations.

01.00 - Watch below unless called for breakdown.

It was after moving to stern trawlers that I realised the great amount of technical knowledge I needed to maintain all this equipment. As we had moved forward from electronic files and equipment to modern transistor and semi-conductor units, I thought I must get up to date with this technology. So when I had some time in dock I enrolled at the College of Technology in Queens Gardens to take a course that enabled me to achieve this.

With the extra electronics' knowledge that I gained, I was far more capable of carrying out the varied maintenance and repair jobs on board. But apart from that there were other instances when this knowledge proved beneficial.

On a voyage to Greenland we were fishing the normal banks when a large Norwegian stern fisher on his maiden voyage to Greenland had a problem with his radar and echo sounders.

He called any British stern fisher in the area and asked if one of their radio officers could assist him.

The Skipper asked me if I was willing to go across to him. I agreed and the Norwegians sent a boat to pick me up and take me to him. When I boarded the vessel I was surprised to see equipment similar to ours. We cleared the faults on the radar and sounders. The vessel carried a radio officer but he had no experience of the equipment.

On another voyage we were fishing off Iceland when our own vessel, the Junella, had similar trouble. So once again I was transferred across by boat to assist in clearing the fault, then taken back to the Northella.

Yet another incident happened while we were fishing in South Newfoundland. The Portuguese vessel,

Robert Baillie

Antonio Pascall had been fitted with a Decca Plotter. This machine operated in conjunction with Decca Navigator but again the radio officer had no experience with either, so once again a boat was sent for me and I went on board to demonstrate to them how to operate the plotter. After the demonstration I had a very enjoyable lunch with the grateful crew, before a boatman rowed me, along with a huge bottle of Portuguese red wine, back to the Northella.

With plenty of time on board to study I had the satisfaction of moving with the times and keeping up with the constantly changing technology.

Another duty that the radio officer normally had to do was looking after the bond. The bond was a small shop on board that sold various commodities including cigarettes, tobacco, cigars, sweets, chocolate, crisps, lemonade, plus beer and spirits, all of course on ration.

I was also in charge of looking after the 'cinema' that we had on board.

We carried a projector and a dozen films that we showed to the crew in their messroom during their 'off watch' periods. That was a summary of my duties…

The crew

Here was the backbone of the ship's workforce the fishermen engaged in deck work and factory work. Many were the same men who had come up from the rough old sidewinder days. Although there was more luxury on these vessels the work was just as hard.

The crew worked watches for 24 hours a day, from 00.00 hours to 06.00 hours, 06.00 hours to 12:00 hours, 12.00 hours to 18:00 hours and 18.00 to midnight.

During a typical day those men engaged in the paying and hauling of the net, and were on deck in all weathers. As soon as the trawl was payed away, they would proceed to the factory where they would gut the fish.

It was then thrown into the washing machine, then sent by a conveyor belt to another part of the factory and placed into bins. The fish was then put into slotted freezers and after the prescribed time was removed as frozen blocks of fish, each weighing 112lbs. Finally, these were sent down in the lift and stowed in the fish hold. A full ship would return home with over 12,000 blocks on board.

This process was logged on special sheets on the factory deck and every night at 23:00 hours the factory manager brought me a report of the total number of blocks we had on board and how many blocks had been produced during that day.

I coded up this information and once again dispatched it by Morse code to our office in Hull, which then had a complete dossier on our voyage.

As well as communication with the shore by Morse code we had an additional means of communication by telephone. Our modern transmitters were fitted to transmit radio telephone, R/T. This meant that by contacting Portishead Radio on high frequency, we could telephone to anywhere in Britain. Here now was a means of crewmen being able to make telephone calls to their wives and families ashore from any position in the Arctic or off the Canadian or Greenland coasts.

Of course the main source of communication between the crew and their wives and girlfriends was still by telegram. This was still a daily occurrence, with the radio officer often smiling at some that were received...

Saturday, May 17 1969
08.00 – Sailed, bound for the North Norwegian coast.

Robert Baillie

Wednesday May 21
08.00 - Passed North Cape, Norway
10.45 - Commenced fishing Nord Kyn - first haul 300 baskets. Then to a position 23 miles off Omgang, average 150 baskets per haul, then to position Kjolneb, bearing 250° - 11 miles and Makkur 190° - 17 miles, averaging 150 to 250 baskets per haul. Fished from North Cape to Vardo, plenty of fish.

Wednesday, June 18
05.45 - We are bound to Hull with a full ship, landed 550 tons.

Saturday, June 28
Sailed again for the Norwegian coast.

Wednesday, July 2
12:30 - Commenced fishing North Cape, here 400 to 500 baskets per haul. Very good fishing. Stor Stappen 14 miles off, lot of fish North Cape to Yjelmsoy, up to 600 baskets per haul.
Position Helsnes 182° 17 miles off, lot of fish 300 to 500 baskets per haul. We are now laid clearing fish.

Friday, July 25
01.00 - Bound for Hull with a full ship. We will be in dock until September.

Now it was touring around time at home, starting with a trip to Blackpool, then Whitby, the Moors and Scotland. The weather was very warm so these were followed by frequent visits to Bridlington and Scarborough, in fact practically anywhere on the Yorkshire map.

My daughter had now reached the age of 17 and had passed her driving test at the first attempt. So it was bye-bye to my car and hello petrol bill. But it was great news as now she could drive her mother around while I was away at sea.

WAITING FOR THE TIDE

Friday, September 19
Midnight - Sailed once again for Norwegian coast.

Tuesday, September 23
22.30 - Commenced south-southwest Cape Bull, average here was 80 baskets per haul but our scheduled reports showed heavy fishing once again from Vardo eastwards to Kildin Bank.

Sunday, September 28
08.30 - Bound to White Sea.

Tuesday, September 30
Fishing Tsypt Navalock to Kildin Bank, Russian coast. Steamed to position 70.50ºN 40.20ºE. Up to 200 baskets per haul.

Friday, October 31
01.00 - Bound for Hull as our worldwide fishing information reported Newfoundland, Labrador and Greenland very slack.

Monday, November 3
North Sea, passed Staflo oil rig – docked in Hull and landed 411 tons.

Tuesday, November 11
08.00 left dock bound for Bear Island.

Saturday, November 15
Commenced fishing west of Bear Island, lot of fish here in 250 fathoms.

Monday, November 25
19:00 - Fishing slackened off at Bear Island, good reports of Splitzbergen, now steaming there.
Lot of fish, ice point 090° - commenced fishing Spitzbergen 77.30ºN. 11.20ºE.
Good fishing but very cold, the temperature is -19°.
Now position Suffolk Point bearing 050°T. 400 fathoms, up to 300 baskets. Now severe frost with pancake ice field sighted.

Sunday, November 30
18:00 - Proceeding south, lot of ice now and a severe

frost, now steaming to North Cape, Norway. Now at 72° 14 N. 24° E. - average 70 to 100 baskets - 160 to 180 fathoms. The weather has increased to a westerly force 9. Dodging into Yjelmsoy. We are now short of water and bound into Hammerfest for water.

Tuesday, December 16

Have left Hammerfest and now fishing at a position off Teistengrunn, North Norway, average 100 baskets, mostly coley.

Friday, December 19

Left 71° 10 N. 18.12 E. bound for Hull, 11,000 blocks - pity the frost and ice at Spitzbergen drove us out, it was good fishing there. Eventually in the North Sea, weather southwest storm all the way.

We were now in dock over Christmas but 1970 was to throw up more challenges for our industry, starting with the 'Fishermen's Strike'...

CHAPTER 9
EXPERIMENTS & INNOVATION

The 1970s commenced with the stoppage of all trawlers going to sea due to a fishermen's dispute with the trawler owners when all the Hull fishermen came out on strike. This was something I never thought could happen but it was a fact. No ship sailed from Hull for the duration of the strike, which meant that I was at home for over three months.

Unlike the trawler crews who were employed by the owners, marine companies employed the radio officers. The two main ones were Marconi Marine and Redifon Marine, which I was with. We had no part in the dispute, so while I was at home for all this time, I once again took the opportunity to attend college to study more about modern electronics.

During the dispute the owners used the 'break' to get their ships serviced and re-painted.

We sailed again in March 1970 in Northella with a new skipper, Les Fewster, bound for the Norwegian coast. When we arrived at Skomvaer and commenced fishing, there was not much fish so once again we continued to the old hunting grounds of the North Cape.

Here the fishing was reasonable but heavy fishing was reported at Nord Kyn, so we steamed there. It was very good fishing at Nord Kyn with a first haul of 180 to 200 baskets.

We then steamed nearer to the limit line but it was too risky there with a gunboat patrolling along the line so we kept off.

We fished the same area up to Wednesday, April 22 but we then required water and oil so we steamed to Honningsvag, docking at 14:00 hours. Here we met Mr

Robert Baillie

Kaare Richter Hanson, an agent for Hull, Grimsby and the new trawling firm from the Tyne, The Ranger Trawling Company, who was well known to every skipper sailing the White Sea.

On Friday, April 24 at 05.00 hours we left for home with a full ship and landed 514 tons.

The next voyage, up to October 9, 1970 we again fished the Norwegian coast. This area had been exceptionally good to us with more or less a full ship after each trip. But gradually the fish was going from that area, no doubt most of it had been caught. It looked like we would have to return to our old grounds in Newfoundland, Labrador and Greenland...

1970

Wednesday, October 21

11:30am - We sailed for Newfoundland and commenced fishing position 52º40 N. 52º00 W. but very slack fishing steamed to Le Grand Nord, Grand Banks, only averaging 40 baskets.

Sunday, November 1

13:00 - We entered the Port of St John's for fuel, food and water.

Monday, November 2

07.00 - Left St John's bound for Greenland. We then fished every bank on the west coast of Greenland from Holsteinburg to Cape Farewell but we were hampered by southeast winds up to storm force 10.

Sunday December 6

We had to give in and were bound for home.

Saturday, December 19

11.00 - Sailed for Greenland and commenced fishing on Christmas Eve

Thursday, December 24

At Nanortalik, Greenland.

Christmas Day

Fishing Nanortalik and on December 28, 29 and 30 we

were laid, had stopped fishing for bad weather and ice.

Thursday December 31

Fishing again, weather had improved but a lot of ice around. Very good fishing, up to 300 baskets per haul, all cod.

1971

Friday, January 1

Happy New Year - Still fishing Nanortalik surrounded by ice but we still managed a wee dram and a chorus of 'Auld Lang Syne'. Then as I gazed at the shore of this frozen wasteland I thought of the Eskimos that I had met in Godthab years before and how they would be enjoying their New Year. But then it was back to the fishing. Fish meant money and of course we could always do with plenty of it.

Friday, January 8

We are now surrounded with ice with no chance of fishing at Greenland so we are now bound for Iceland.

Saturday, January 9

Passed Cape Farewell steaming across Denmark Strait.

Monday, January 11

Commenced fishing off Isafiord, Iceland - weather bad.

Tuesday, January 12

Stopped fishing, weather too bad.

Wednesday, January 13

Laid under Ritur Huk, weather bad.

Thursday, January 14

Now fishing again Hali Bank, good fishing.

Friday, January 15

Under Ritur Huk again, weather freezing hard and the winds are northeast force 9.

Sunday, January 17

Fishing again.

Tuesday, January 19

Ice pack, temperature is $-12°$ - back under Ritur Huk -

north-northeast storm kept coming. Some good fishing at Hali Bank when weather permitted.

Tuesday, January 26

Weather increasing now - wind northeast force 9. We are near the ice field and temperatures are -19°. We remained at Hali Bank going into Isafiord when winds were gale to storm force for shelter then out again when they decreased. Good fishing when permitted and if the ice field doesn't come over the fishing grounds.

Sunday, January 31

Ice field too close - bound home with 8,340 blocks, 363 tons,

Tuesday, February 2

21:00 - Bound for Aberdeen for fuel.

Wednesday, February 3

In Aberdeen for fuel

Thursday, February 4

12.00 – Docked at St Andrews Dock.

Thursday, February 11

A week later we sailed again for Newfoundland where we fished the full voyage at the Flemish Gap. The fishing was very good but on Saturday, February 27 we became fast on the sea bottom, parted our starboard side warp and lost 26 lengths of wire. So bound into St John's for new wire.

Thursday, March 4

Back at Flemish Gap. Fished until Wednesday, March 30, position 46.25ºN. 46ºW. At 15:30 we left for home, thick fog, landed 10,400 blocks, 497 tons.

The voyages continued and from March to December 1971 we fished all positions in the Arctic from the Grand Banks, Newfoundland to Labrador, Greenland, Iceland, the Norwegian coast and the White Sea. The average landings were 400 to 500 tons.

WAITING FOR THE TIDE

Our main battle was with the elements, the common enemy of the Arctic fishermen, storm force 12 winds and ice fields.

During my voyages to the Nova Scotia and Newfoundland coasts, I was engaged in new experiments with electronic navigation equipment. Working for the White Fish Authority in Hull, I was given the job of testing Loran C. The difference here was that where Loran A and B had only two stations transmitting from shore, Loran C had three stations, making it a more accurate long-range navigation unit.

So day and night, I took the Loran B position, the Loran C position, the Decca position and the radar position if in range of land. All these readings were logged on special sheets issued from shore and the results returned to the White Fresh Authority on docking. All these results were then computed. This experiment was to ascertain how accurate Loran C was and if it was the future of navigation aids?

1971

Thursday, April 15,
08.00 hours - sailed for Iceland as reports of plenty of ice in Greenland.

Saturday, April 17
Slack fishing reports Iceland so still bound Greenland.

Monday, April 19
Reports of very heavy ice at Greenland so from position 50 942 N. 2445 W. bound for Iceland.

Tuesday, April 20
Shot at Eldey Bank, Iceland then to Hali Bank. Weather has got very bad at Iceland, once again steaming to Greenland.

Monday, April 26
Still steaming Davis Strait plenty of ice, commenced Lyllas Bank but on Sunday, May 2 conditions too bad

at Greenland, steaming south to Labrador.

Tuesday, May 4

09.00 hours - position 55.01 N. 52.29 W. Labrador but unworkable, too much ice so steaming again to Woolfall Bank then in position 47.15 N. 51.35 W. shot our trawl, as high as 120 baskets per haul. Fished this area till Thursday, June 10 when we left for home 9,845 blocks and 1,415 single cod.

Thursday, June 17

Docked in Hull

Saturday, June 26

08.00 - Bound for Newfoundland once again, fished Grand Banks from Friday, July 2 to Tuesday, August 10 when we returned to Hull and docked with 300 tons.

At the end of August once again bound for Greenland with skipper Frank Dunning, fished from Fyllas Bank to Nanartalik but hopeless ice and slack fishing.

Saturday, September 11

Passing Cape Farewell bound for Iceland

Tuesday, September 14

Commenced fishing at Vikurall, Iceland then Hali Bank. Here I transferred by boat to the Junella to repair his radar. We fished Hali Bank until Sunday, September 26 but weather became very bad so we steamed to the east side to Kjolsen Bank, very little fish so steamed to Glettinganes.

Tuesday, September 28

We had to go into Seydisfiord for a propeller fan repair

Thursday, September 30

Left Seydisfiord for fishing grounds and fished from Glettinganes to Bullnose, The Kidney, Hari-Kari Bank and Workingman's Bank.

Friday, October 8

Bound for Hull, Iceland was no place for a freezer, not enough fish there.

WAITING FOR THE TIDE

We docked in Hull on Sunday, October 10 so had a few days at home with the family. But as you can see, there was no mariner who did as much time at sea as a freezer crewman.

Monday, October 18
05.30 - Sailed for the White Sea
Friday, October 22
Commenced fishing north of North Cape bank but weather bad, steaming to a position 73.15ºN. 32.40ºE. Very poor fishing right up to Wednesday, November 3.
Wednesday, November 3
Steamed to Murmansk coast, Russia, now fishing in position 70.10N 32.50E - it is freezing hard now -9º below and slack fishing. Very good reports of plaice fishing at Cape Cherni on the east Russian coast. We decided to try plaice fishing and steamed to Cape Cherni, here averaged about 30 blocks of plaice but this was no good for a large freezer so steamed back.
Tuesday, November 23
Commenced fishing 72ºN 32.44ºE.

Here we were going to experiment with the Pelagic Trawl. This new type of trawl was designed so that you could fish at depths above the sea bottom in contrast to the old trawl where it had to be on the bottom.

The unique feature with this trawl was the cable winch. On the headline of the trawl was fixed a transducer connected by an electronic cable via its winch to the bridge echo sounder. The cable on this winch was payed away with the trawl controlled by a unit on the bridge containing press buttons '1', '2' and '3'. The other button was for stop, and was only used when the trawl and cable was inboard. You payed away on '1', the transducer's signal showed up the ground

Robert Baillie

rope of the trawl as well as the bottom. You could then pick up this ground rope or foot rope as it was known on your echo sounder and by increasing or decreasing your speed you could raise or lower the net to the depth you were going to fish.

Not only that but fish echoes could be observed entering your trawl. The cable winch would automatically unwind or wind up slack cable when towing. When hauling the net you could use the buttons to make the winch haul the electronic cable in with the trawl winch hauling the net in.

There was a snag that if the electronic cable parted, you immediately lost sight of your trawl on the echo sounder and you had to haul the net in immediately.

Repairing the electronic cable was of course one of my duties. The two broken ends would be hauled up to the upper deck where I had my box of repairing gadgets ready.

The cable had an inner and outer conductor. You cut the rubber outer covering first, then the wire mesh outer conductor, then the plastic covering the inner conductor.

Then with the aid of a small metal tube, a crimping tool and some insulation tape, the cable could be quickly repaired and made as good as new.

Finally, the repaired cable was tested with the echosounder and if the signal was okay, then off we went.

The cable was undoubtedly a crucial part of the entire fishing operation. Even when it appeared that there was no fish to be caught, we often had huge successes with our high lift trawl. Technology was progressing on every voyage.

I have included numerous details about the electronic equipment on board fishing vessels to show the huge steps forward in modern technology used by the fishing industry from my steamship days of 1947 to the modern trawlers of 1971. It was certainly remarkable how well the fishing industry and the entire crews of the vessels, kept up with modern techniques.

Whenever I had a few weeks at home I always tried to get back to Hull's College of Technology and keep up to date with the ever changing 'electronic world'. The man who said, 'I know it all,' to me was either a fool or had stood still in time. I would always keep on learning.

On Saturday, November 27 at 01.00, we were bound for home and thanks to our Pelagic trawl we'd had a good voyage. We docked in Hull on Thursday, December 2 and received the great news that we were going to be at home for Christmas and New Year.

So now, I was looking forward to the festive period, when the only ice that I'd be seeing was a cube or two in my drink.

I had more than one thing to celebrate during the holidays. On December 23 it was our wedding anniversary. 21 years married, I could hardly believe it. The time had flown by so quickly and plenty of water had passed under my feet during those years.

The other event that Rita and I had to celebrate was that we were now grandparents. Yes, I was a granddad. Our granddaughter Lisa was one year old in January 1972.

For the majority of this book I deal mostly with the fishing side of my life. I spent that long at sea that I seem to have forgotten about a lot of the family side of the story.

My daughter Patricia for instance was now 19 years old. But I had never been at home long enough to see her grow up. The time we had together was limited

Robert Baillie

to the time I spent ashore. I was not alone in this of course, as it was the same for all deep-sea fishermen. So you had to salute the wives who acted as both mother and father bringing up their children.

Now however, I was going to enjoy the great excitement of being at home for Christmas and the New Year. And with my granddaughter involved as well, I was going to get the best Christmas tree, decorations and presents in the land. And for once the crunch of the ice and the freezing temperatures would be forgotten.

We celebrated our anniversary and when Christmas at last arrived, I remember how wonderful it was getting the tree ready and putting all the presents around it. And on Christmas Eve it was even better as Rita and I watched our granddaughter waiting for her first Christmas Day to appear. Now to the shoreman, this would be just another annual event but for others like me, where being at home at this time of year was a novelty, this was really something to remember.

On Christmas Day we enjoyed a lovely Christmas dinner with turkey and all the trimmings. But there was something different. No violent moving of the table, no screaming storm outside and no pack ice. This was certainly heaven. Then it was time to play with Lisa's toys and to see the excitement that shone all over her happy face.

It was only then that I thought about how the studying and the years of hard work at sea had enabled me to earn the money and provide the best for my family.

This was certainly a period to remember. And although I had a great time at home over the festive season, it was over all too soon. But I had a granddaughter now and I was determined that she would have the best of everything. So I had to get to sea again, when once more I would be sailing in wild and treacherous waters to bring fish to the people...

We sailed again for the Norwegian coast. It was a bit of a rough voyage with bad weather up to Skomvaer but this was expected at that time of year. There was very little fish around Skomvaer so we decided to steam to Bear Island. We fished there for about forty hours but bad weather and freezing conditions forced us to go elsewhere, so we steamed to the North Cape.

Fishing on the Norwegian coast was moderate so you were always prepared for a long voyage. But fishing the Norwegian coast also brought some lighter moments on board the Northella. One of these took place while we were in Honningsvag for a small repair.

One of the films we had on board for this voyage was called 'Bedknobs and Broomsticks'. It was a great film for children so while in port we invited the children from Honningsvag to come on board to watch it. The cook made some buns and jellies for them and they all had a great time eating and enjoying the film.

We fished up to March, it was not heavy fishing by any means, just steady for most of the voyage. Meanwhile I was still engaged in my meteorological duties sending in my daily observations, including the direction and force of the wind, cloud formation, precipitation, barometer reading and temperature reading, direct to Bracknell

When our fishing voyage finished, we had about 350 tons on board and returned to Hull. So ended our first voyage of 1972...

While we were back in dock I had a telephone call concerning my weather observations. It was to inform me that I had been given an award for the work I had done.

This turned out to be a beautiful Atlas. Inside the book was written: Awarded by the Director General of the Meteorological Office to Mr R Baillie, MT Northella, as an acknowledgement of his valuable work at sea over the years.

I still hold the book with pride today, as it shows that a freezer trawler did more than just fish. It was also a weather observing ship for the Arctic.

While in dock I was given another duty to carry out. A company of schoolboys and girls were arriving in Hull from a school in the West Riding of Yorkshire to visit the fish dock and come aboard a large freezer stern trawler and I had the job of showing them around the vessel. There were twenty-five pupils, around 14 or 15 years old, so first of all I went to the small shop in our road for twenty-five small bottles of lemonade and a box of fifty packets of crisps. I loaded them into my car and I then went back to meet the schoolchildren and their teacher. They spent quite an educational few hours on board and were most surprised at the vastness of the ship and of the dangerous conditions in the Arctic where the fish that they bought in their fish shops was caught. But then after a bottle of lemonade and two packets of crisps each, they departed.

We sailed again in April 1972, this time bound for the Murmansk coast fishing grounds. The skipper for this voyage was Billy Wilson. Bill was one of the winners of the 'Silver Cod Trophy', which was awarded to the sidewinder landing the most fish over a certain period of time.

There was a bit of controversy here as the larger sidewinders had an advantage, being faster and having more fish capacity. This competition therefore sometimes meant that quality and size gave way to the amount caught.

We had an example of this one voyage when we arrived at the west of Bear Island and came across one of the Silver Cod front runners. She was laid with a deckload of fish and we thought that we were in with a chance. But after two tows and two hauls of fish we could not believe it. The fish was far too small for us so we steamed on but it was a fierce competition. Later we learned that the rules had changed and the winner was the one with the most fish sold when landed.

Anyway it was something new in the 60s and a great honour for a skipper and a firm to win. Marr's was more often than not amongst the front runners.

We steamed on for the Murmansk coast and commenced fishing at Kildin. This was the Soviet Union's northerly naval base area, the area where in the early 1960s I had taken part in what was described as 'observing the movements of warships and submarines'. But this had all finished. It was no longer necessary with all the modern ways that were available to 'watch' each other.

We commenced fishing just outside the fishing limit at Kildin, which was moderate to good. While operating there on our own, a Russian gunboat approached us. He hoisted a flag, which when we looked it up in the international codebook, read 'Follow me'. But as we were outside the line we didn't take much notice of him.

He went away steaming towards shore but a later on, a much larger gunboat appeared and he didn't mess about with the order, 'Follow me on the course indicated'. That was out to sea! He took us was well out and then steamed back inside.

We thought we had better stay away from the limit for a while but not much later we were back in it again. This time there was no trouble so we carried on fishing until May 20 and then left for home. It was a moderate to good voyage and we continued our voyages to the Murmansk coast throughout 1972.

Robert Baillie

In September 1972 I experienced one of the saddest times of my life.

My father had retired and had moved with my mother and sister to Aberdeen. It was my usual custom to phone them the night before I sailed. So as I was due to sail on the morning tide in the Northella, I phoned at around 9pm to find that my mother had been taken to hospital having suffered a stroke and had later died.

I then had to contact someone at Marr's to inform them that I couldn't sail as planned. This they naturally understood and the next day I made my way to Aberdeen by train as the Northella sailed without me.

Here was the passing of a great lady who gave everything to all her family. She would be sadly missed.

In November 1972 I returned from Aberdeen. The Northella was at sea once again, so with a few weeks to spare I enrolled at the Hull College of Technology to again further my studies of advanced electronics. This was most important as new ships were being built with the most modern of electronic equipment and studying the new innovations in this field was a must.

After a while Northella arrived home and I prepared to sail in her again but we had news that this next voyage could be the last in this great ship as Northella was going to be sold to a South African company.

It would be a sad day if that happened.

But it was correct. Our next voyage was our last in the Northella. Our old skipper Les Fewster was in charge, sailing alongside my good friend and chief engineer Jim Powdrell and myself, who had been together for all those years in Northella through virtually every danger imaginable.

We had worked together on all sorts of breakdowns. But there was one incident that reminded me of how vulnerable to the oceans even the more modern ships were.

It was always a fear that when the fish hatch door on deck was opened to take the fish down, it could also 'take a sea down' if the weather was very bad.

Northella had lots of electric equipment aft side and one day this happened. We took a sea down the hatch flooding the entire steering compartment. The water rose completely covering our electronic steering motors and wiping them out.

So now we had no electronic steering. The skipper had to operate the vessel by hand. Steering was a difficult manoeuvre on a big stern trawler.

Our first move was to get new motors sent out. This was arranged and one of our vessels leaving Hull brought out the motors to us and transferred them at sea. But when we received them we found the motor shafts were too long.

Jim immediately used his engineering skills to cut them to the correct length, re-thread the ends and fit them into position. I then took over the rewiring to the motors and soon we were mobile again with our electronic steering fully restored.

When we arrived home and docked, Jim Powdrell and I sat in my cabin with a bottle of whiskey almost in silence. It was like preparing to leave an old home.

Jim was informed that he would be going out as chief engineer on the Northella to South Africa. I thought I would be going as well but that wasn't the case. I was informed that I would be joining the brand-new freezer, Cordella. It was currently being built in Wallsend, Newcastle and I would be up there until it was ready to sail on its maiden voyage under Captain Ron Boughen.

I signed off the Northella for the last time and bid a final farewell to the crew members whom I had sailed

Robert Baillie

with for all those years.

Now I was going to have some time at home before going to Wallsend. I had a pile of jobs to do in the house and garden, which had accumulated while I had been away but I was also able to take the family out on trips to different venues.

The day soon arrived when we were going to Wallsend for the first view of our new vessel and to get to know all about our new ship.

We left by bus in the afternoon and arrived at our hotel in Whitley Bay at teatime.

We were booked in for the night and prepared to be down at the dock in Wallsend at 7.30 the next morning.

The evening was a get-together in the lounge bar as we were going to be a new crew meeting the captain, mate, bosun, chief engineer and cook etc. The Captain, Ron Boughen, I knew well from my early days and he had sailed with us as first mate a few years before.

So it was drinks all round.

The next morning immediately after breakfast a bus came to the hotel to take us to the dock for our first sighting of Cordella. We were going to be on the dock till 18.00 before returning to the hotel.

We arrived at Wallsend dock at 7.30am and the moment we emerged from the bus there she was – the Cordella.

As I gazed at the fantastic looking ship, I thought back 25 years to when I had stepped aboard my first trawler, a coal-fired, steam ship. And now this. I took a deep breath and walked confidently towards her...

CHAPTER 10
CORDELLA

When I boarded the vessel, it was crawling with workmen getting it ready. I entered a door below the bridge and made my way along a corridor. On my port side was the entrance up onto the bridge and on my starboard side was a small corridor with one door marked 'Captain' and further along another door marked 'Radio Officer'. I opened the second door and looked in and the sight that met my eyes was one that I could only describe as one of sheer luxury.

Here was my own cabin and dayroom, with my bunk, a set of drawers, a blue upholstered locker, a table with a pull-out lamp and drawers, a cupboard for suits etc., and a fully fitted plush blue carpet.

On the walls was a cupboard with a glass front, a chrome steam heater and a chrome speaker on an oak base for the radio entertainment and ship's orders. Then to top it all I had my own bathroom with a sink, toilet, shower and another chrome steam heater.

Next door was the radio room, fitted with the most modern of communications' equipment including a high-powered transmitter, a standby R/T transmitter and two receivers, all digitally controlled, and a music and tannoy system covering all the ship's quarters.

Moving to the bridge, there were twin radars, twin echo sounders, automatic steering, a tannoy system for the ship's orders, a VHF direction finder, a Decca receiver and Decca plotter, Loren for navigation and a winch control room. This little room with a panel of buttons actually controlled our main winch for paying and hauling the trawl away.

The winchman would work inside now. There would be no paying away behind an open winch with

143

Top: Cordella   Bottom: Me, working on Cordella

gale force, freezing winds in his face, no frozen hands on iron controls or icy seas crashing around him.

I next made my way down aft. Here was the officers' mess room, the galley and the crew's messroom, which included a projector room for film-shows and a TV that could be used over on the Canadian-Newfoundland coast.

The factory was also very modern with its belt fed machinery from the fish gutting area to the freezers. This ship was different from the rest re its electrical output, the old type being DC whereas this ship had AC output points. They were handy for crewmembers bringing their own portable radios and TVs etc. To me this was the ultimate fishing vessel.

For the next week or so we would be on this vessel everyday, learning all about the new radios, transmitters, echo sounders, radars and navigation aids. Where all the switches were, the wiring and the power sources. It was an endless task but it had to be done to be efficient at sea.

On reading about all this luxury and new innovations you might think that being a fisherman wasn't that bad a job. But don't forget this same ship and men were still going to serve in icebound waters, freezing storms and pack ice. The danger was still there at all times.

The weeks went by and eventually the day arrived when this ship was finished and ready for sea. So then it was back home for a few days before we received orders to return by bus again to Wallsend for sea trials.

We arrived at the dock, boarded Cordella and it was cast off for the trials. What is ship this, steaming up and down and carrying out speed trials off the Tyne.

I also utilised the trials to test the radio transmitter and receiver with Cullercoats Radio. It was all working perfectly. After the trials there were one or two jobs to clear it up before sailing on our first voyage. Then it was the bus back home and a last run out with the family before our maiden voyage…

When the day that we were due to sail finally arrived, it began with the usual bus ride to Wallsend. We loaded all our sea gear aboard and cast off. This was it!

Slowly we made our way out into the North Sea, then headed north to Pentland Firth.

As Cordella made her way effortlessly through the waves at a steady 17 knots I again thought what a great ship she was. Then I recalled my first ever sea voyage, on the coal-fired steam ship, Chrysoberyl. Times had certainly changed.

Soon we were in the Atlantic, bound for the Grand Banks, Newfoundland, sailing along in the beautiful, summer weather. The vessel was fitted with automatic steering, so there was no helmsman just a standby manual steering wheel in case of an electronic failure. It was also fitted with a variable pitch propeller. This was the master control for 'pelagic fishing' a system that most fishing vessels would use in the future.

As we navigated along our track our great ship's speed was shown. We seemed to being flying along. In my radio room I sat back in my specially built, black upholstered chair and my thoughts again returned to my steam sailing days.

After a few days we arrived at our first fishing bank and prepared to fish. As everything was new it was going to take a few days to get used to all the gear.

One must give credit to all the fishing crews. They had moved forward with all the new technology without any schooling but had quickly adapted to all the new fishing techniques.

We payed away the trawl. The winchman was in

his little control box on the bridge with a wide lookout window and even driven electrically window wipers to keep his view clear.

He definitely didn't need an oil frock. But here on the Newfoundland banks we were going to meet a new enemy to add to our list of hazards – fog! And when I say fog, this was the worst. It lasted for weeks on end when you never saw a clear view of what was around you So imagine shooting your trawl away at full speed among a huge crowd of other fishing vessels.

This is where radar was most important. If your radar broke down you stopped fishing. My job was to make sure that never happened and the radar was always working. The electronic part of this vessel whether it was radars, echo sounders, navigation aids, gyros, radios and transmitters was my responsibility. The time was coming where the radio officer would also be recognised as an electronics officer and this would mean going back to college for a long while to attain this proficiency. This I was prepared to do even though I was over 50 because as the saying goes, You're never too old to learn…

We carried on fishing in the dense fog. There were plenty of boats in the area as 'Le Grand Nord' was a bank well patronised by fishing vessels of all nationalities, including West and East German, Portuguese, Polish, Russian and French. This time of year fishing was generally slack and you found it took longer to fill the ship up. But anyway we were all getting the feel of the new vessel.

The Marr's colours of yellow and red on the funnel made their ships stand out, so being brand-new our vessel got quite a few glances as we passed by.

We fished on relentlessly, up and down the banks, day after day.

Robert Baillie

It was now time to go into St John's in Newfoundland to refuel and get stores, so I called St John's radio to book a pilot and give them our ETA.

We hauled our net and dropped the fish down into the factory to be processed, then cleaned the ship ready for docking. We then telephoned our agent Humphries what we required, then proceeded to St John's, picked up a pilot outside the harbour and entered the port. As we were re-fuelling we berthed across on the other side of the harbour from the town, a fair distance if you were going to do some shopping and planned to walk there. While we were there, I was certainly going into the town, as I wanted to get a Canadian doll for my granddaughter Lisa.

The weather was very hot, around 80° degrees, so the first mate, Eddie Fuller and I decided to walk round into town. I hunted through the shops for a doll and came across one, an Eskimo dressed in traditional clothes.

We then called into a bar restaurant, the 'Starboard Quarter' for a cold beer and a dram of Scotch. The young girl who served us asked, 'Are you off that yellow ship at the other side of the harbour?'

We replied that we were.

'That's a beautiful looking boat,' she remarked.

When it was time to leave, Eddie said to me, 'Bails, we are not walking back round there in this heat, and with my poor feet,' and he got up and ordered a taxi back to the ship.

Back on board I met my old friend Humphries the agent, who as usual was enjoying a mug of English tea with two sugars.

When we had re-fuelled and taken the stores onboard, the crew had a short time ashore and then it was time to sail again.

In St Johns the weather was lovely, sunny and

clear with not a hint of any fog, but on the Grand Bank the dense fog persisted. With everyone back on board, we set off for the last remaining days' fishing of the voyage.

We must not forget what the crew's duties were on the Cordella. Although all was mostly factory work, it was still a tough job working in there. It wasn't like a shore factory, this one rolled around day and night.

The crew were paying trawls away, hauling trawls, putting the fish down into the factory and mending the torn nets. In the factory, the fish was gutted and the cod-liver oil was processed. The fish was then put onto moving belts that took it to the freezers where it was eventually formed into large blocks. These blocks of fish were then transported down to the fish hold in a lift. And all this took place as the ship rolled around to an extent determined by the weather conditions.

This was a big ship but remember the sea has no regard for size and when the crew were on the open deck those same freezing seas and winds were still there. The sea coming up the ramp of a stern trawler could easily swamp the deck in seconds, washing away everything before it. This included men, so one had to treat the sea with respect.

One remarkable thing with Cordella was that we were able to convert seawater into fresh water for domestic use. In the old days you filled up with fresh water which was used for all purposes. When you were short of water you had to go into the nearest port to take more fresh water on board. With this special apparatus on Cordella however, we could make fresh from seawater although drinking water was still stored in a separate tank.

Another thing that I always remembered about Cordella was how knowledgeable the chief engineer and staff were regarding all the new techniques that were on the vessel. Our chief Don Jarrett was in this bracket of first-class engineers. Things had certainly changed since the day that I joined the fishing fleet with its coal-fired steam ships and firemen breaking their backs shovelling coal into furnaces…

Our maiden voyage was coming to an end. Within a few days we had finished fishing so it was clean the factory, then clean the ship fore and aft and make course for home after another sixty days at sea.

With fine weather we were soon across the Atlantic. The first land we saw was the Butt of Lewis, then we continued on through the Pentland Firth.

Here, I recall a little incident that occurred as we were leaving the Firth and approaching Aberdeen. I was called early in the morning as a ship was flashing to us. Getting my Aldis light I answered his message that simply asked, 'What is the name of your ship and where are you bound?'

I answered, 'MT Cordella and we are bound for Hull from Newfoundland.'

The reply that I received back was short but was certainly a surprising one, it read, 'This is the Royal Ship Britannia. Good voyage.'

We assumed that the ship was either carrying the Queen to Balmoral or picking her up from a stay there.

We then continued down the North Sea coast, passed Flamborough and Spurn to Hull, and docked at the stern freezers' berth. There were many families on the quay waiting to greet husbands, dads and granddads, like myself, as well as sons, boyfriends and the younger crewmembers. The families of these men waited patiently at home for weeks on end praying for their safe return. In the old sidewinder, it was an average of 21 days away but now we were looking at 60 to 70 days. And remember that during this time, wives, girlfriends and children would be constantly aware of the great dangers encountered by their men-folk in this most dangerous of professions.

Once again I sat in my modern cabin and enjoyed a beer and a dram. This time though, it was not to remember the final voyage of a ship but to celebrate the first voyage of a new one. Life seemed great...

After we had landed our voyage, I remained on board for quite a while clearing up the 'snags' because as it was the ship's first voyage there were naturally one or two problems to sort out. After that though it was 'family time'.

Once again it was time to get the car out and set off with my wife, daughter and granddaughter for a few days out in the countryside. We spent a lot of days from dawn to dusk out in the country. The scenery was very different compared with having just the cruel sea around you and there were certainly no icebergs or pack ice on the Yorkshire Moors.

One of the first things that I did was to give Lisa the Eskimo doll that I had purchased for her in St John's. Many years later, I'm pleased to say that we still have that doll.

When Cordella had passed her tests it was time to refuel and prepare for our next voyage.

This time we were bound for the White Sea. It was the voyage before Christmas. We left the dock and followed the same old course to the Norwegian coast, passing Svino, Skomvaer and along the North Cape to a position off the east bank.

We prepared our trawl and commenced fishing, which was very good. We had been informed when we left Hull that we would definitely be home for Christmas but after only a couple of days disaster struck. Early in the morning we heard a loud bang in the

Robert Baillie

engine room and knew immediately that something serious had happened. Our chief engineer informed the captain that we would have to make for the nearest port. This was Kirkenes in Norway, only about seven kilometres from the Russian border. So we limped slowly to Kirkenes and docked alongside a large pier that served the nearby iron ore mine. Kirkenes was only a small place but was well known for its mine where ships from all nations came to trade.

We waited for our superintendent engineer, Mr Arthur Hogan, to arrive by air to survey what the fault was and what damage had been done to our engine. As far as the captain and crew were concerned it was just 'relax and wait to see what happened'.

Mr Hogan arrived and after an inspection we were informed that it looked as though we were going to be there for some time.

The first essential thing that we required was an efficient communication link up as telephoning ashore would have been hazardous because there was no proper telephone facility on the quay. This was where our ship's VHF telephone transmitter and receiver was going to be of immense value.

I called the Norwegian station, Vardo Radio, explaining to him the situation regarding our engine and that many ship to shore calls would be required, especially to Britain. Vardo immediately allocated a channel for us where we could call direct into him whenever required and believe me this ended up a full day's operation.

After a while we were informed that we could be in Kirkenes for anything up to two weeks. Remember that not only Christmas but also winter was approaching with freezing and stormy conditions.

Worse was to follow as we also found out that the engine fault had affected our main winch as the oil had been contaminated with metal filings.

My duty was to ensure constant radio communication with Vardo Radio as other technical personnel would undoubtedly be required. Day after day we remained alongside the iron mine. We could walk into Kirkenes but it was like walking to the North Pole through constant snow blizzards and over ground covered in thick ice. The only thing that we could do was to remain on board ship. But at least we had plenty of repeat film shows to watch.

We were informed that as soon as the engines had been repaired and we could manoeuvre Cordella again we would have to go to Hammerfest for the winch repairs, as Hammerfest was more easily reached by air transport.

While we were waiting in Kirkenes to get the engine fault repaired another amusing incident occurred. A large ship from Glasgow was berthed just ahead of us waiting to take on a cargo of iron ore from the mine. We learned that as they had also been away for some time they had run out of bread and didn't have any facilities on board to bake any. Our cook decided to bake them some fresh breadcakes and the crew also sent them a basket of freshly filleted cod.

When the captain of the vessel sat down to dine that evening with the freshly baked breadcakes and fish, he enquired where they had come from. He was told that they were from the Hull fishing vessel, Cordella. He immediately informed his mate to send an invitation to the Cordella's captain and crew to come aboard for drinks and this was readily accepted.

I spent a great evening chatting with their radio officer over a few drinks and of course had a look round his radio and radar equipment. The crew also had quite a night with the help of 'a beer or two' and a few of them had difficulty getting back in the thick snow.

Robert Baillie

The next morning, as I sat in Kirkenes, I thought of how close it was to the Russian border and about my duty in the early 1960s observing the movements of the northern Soviet fleet. But this had all finished as far as I was concerned. We had been relieved of that duty a few years ago and everything seemed a lot friendlier now.

The game now was patience. December was getting nearer and nearer and we still had Hammerfest to go to yet for winch repairs. The day finally came when the engine repairs were completed. The next thing we could hear was the throb of the engines running. All seemed okay and after a few trials we were ready to move off to Hammerfest. Then came the orders, 'All aboard, make ready for sea,' and we let go from the quay and headed slowly out.

I thanked Vardo Radio for their invaluable assistance during our stay in Kirkenes before we steamed slowly along the Norwegian coast to North Cape making for Hammerfest.

When we berthed, our winch parts that had been flown up from the south, along with a team of Norwegian engineers to fit them, were waiting for us.

Hammerfest of course was a much bigger place than Kirkenes with much more to see ashore. I remember an incident that happened when a member of the crew and I went into Hammerfest one afternoon. We were surprised to see a large crowd in the square singing Christmas carols but they sounded very good so we joined in. The crowd were amused at this and gave us a welcome handshake when they finished.

The Norwegian engineers were extremely efficient and soon had the winch parts fitted and tested. We were then ready to go fishing again.

We didn't have much fishing time left if we were to get home for Christmas, so we left Hammerfest as soon as we could and proceeded back to the grounds off the East Bank where we had left off. The fishing there was moderate to good but the weather was a problem. You could expect this though as it was December with very little daylight in these northern parts. It was also freezing quite hard as well and it was around this position while doing my weather observations that I recorded a temperature on my thermometer of -30°, very cold indeed.

We were informed that we were to fish up to the stated time that would allow us enough time to get home for Christmas. So we fished on and there was quite a bit of excitement on board at the thought of being home for Christmas. It was not often that a freezer man would get to see Christmas at home. We had fished now from East bank to Kildin and back to Kjolnes and Nord Kyn.

This was the end of the voyage. We finished fishing and prepared to clean the ship and the factory. It had been an eventful voyage with our stay in Kirkenes and Hammerfest. But now we were now bound for home. Our course was round the North Cape, along the Norwegian coast passing Tromso and Harstad and eventually Skomvaer and Svino, then into the North Sea, passed Flamborough and Spurn and into the Humber. We docked in Hull and I stepped ashore. Then during my taxi-ride to Hessle, I passed all the houses decorated for Christmas. What a great sight it was. Home at last…

It was certainly a great time for us seafarers, being at home at this time of year. But a bigger surprise was awaiting me when I went back to the dock on settling day.

My company, J Marr, informed me that I would be coming ashore from the Cordella for two voyages. I had been enrolled at the College of Technology in

Top: Cordella's radio room   Bottom: Just hauled

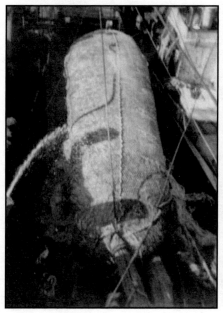

WAITING FOR THE TIDE

Queens Gardens and for over three months I would study and take the Certificate of Advanced Radio and Electronic Engineering, commencing in January 1974.

This to me was great news as I had always been keen to further my education in this advanced technology. So at the age of 50 I was going back to college. I signed off Cordella and prepared myself for the long spell at home. I would be going back in Cordella later and at the time didn't realise that 1974 would be an eventful year for much more than just my unexpected return to the classroom.

Christmas and the New Year were very enjoyable, especially with three to four months ashore and my college course to look forward to. But the break was barely over before my first day back at college was looming.

I bought a new briefcase and some notebooks, pens and pencils. My little granddaughter seemed a bit confused at all of this, Grandad going back to school.

When the first Monday morning finally arrived at Queens Gardens, due to overcrowding in the main college we were transferred to a school annexed to the main college for the duration of our course.

I met the rest of the radio officers in the class, there were eight of us, then the lecturers. We were informed which books we would require and so commenced our first day back at school.

We had nearly four months there, daily from 9am until 4pm, with one hour for lunch taken in the 'Queens' in George Street. Then, after 15 weeks that seemed to fly by, we took our examinations. I passed and was presented with my certificate. This was indeed a great day for me.

The next challenge that faced me however was something very different. I would be taking part in the Icelandic Cod War...

Robert Baillie

CHAPTER 11

QUOTAS & GUNBOATS

After my three months at college, I was now waiting for the return of the Cordella that was still at sea on a fishing voyage. During this period of waiting the situation with the Icelandic dispute had hotted up. Iceland had extended their fishing limit line without International agreement, more or less wiping out the traditional fishing banks where British fishermen had fished for years. The result was that the Royal Navy was brought in to protect our fishing vessels and allow them to fish in their old fishing grounds. This in turn produced an instant reaction from the Icelandic Government resulting in clashes between Icelandic gunboats and the Royal Navy.

I was sent for by the Redifon Marine Radio Company and asked if I would go up to Aberdeen to sail in a small stern trawler 'The Glen Carron' sailing to Iceland while I waited for the Cordella.

This I accepted. I gathered my sea gear together and took a cab to York railway station to catch the London to Aberdeen night train. This was perfect as it meant I would be able to see my father and sister in Aberdeen before sailing. Arriving in Aberdeen I made my way to see my family then went down to the dock to sail and picking out 'The Glen Carron' I went aboard.

This was the smallest stern trawler that you could imagine and by far the smallest I had been on. I made my way to a specially made cabin as normally this boat didn't carry a radio officer, so there was no radio room, all communications were done on the bridge.

The owners of the 'Glen Carron' were P & J Johnstone and were combined with J. Marr, a company that later on I would be working with closely,

WAITING FOR THE TIDE

Klondiking.

We sailed on the next tide and I was more than happy with the crew as they were all Scots. We made our way to Pentland Firth, then westward to Iceland. As we passed the Faroe Islands I thought that the 'Glen Carron' was a fine little sea ship, riding the waves like a little duck despite being much smaller than the huge Cordella.

I had previously had experience with the first Icelandic dispute but this trip was different. When you arrived in Iceland you booked in with a control ship. The fishing areas were termed 'boxes' and you fished inside this limit, guarded by the Royal Navy and the boxes being moved to different positions depending on how good or poor the fishing was.

We arrived on the southeast coast of Iceland, 'booked in' and commenced fishing. This type of stern trawler was more or less a 'fresh fisher'.

So there we were in a box off southeast Iceland, protected by the Royal Navy. But the Icelandic gunboats were not going to just stand by and watch. Their job was to stop foreign trawlers from taking 'their fish' and to make our trips as unproductive as possible. This they did with continuous harassment and attacks, trying to cut our fishing gear with a cutting device that they towed behind them.

Early one morning our alarm klaxon started to sound. The Icelandic gunboat 'Thor' was bearing down on us aiming to cut our gear. A British naval vessel steamed full between 'Thor' and us. All we could see were sparks flying in the air as the two vessels rubbed alongside each other. But it didn't deter us.

We fished for a few days then left for home, escorted out by a Royal Navy vessel.

The weather was pretty poor and we had to put into Faroe to take on fuel before heading home to

Robert Baillie

Aberdeen. Landing our catch on the early market I made my way to Aberdeen station to get the train back to York and then to Hull.

The Cod War was to prove disastrous for the fishing industry in Hull as eventually with terrible political mismanagement, the limit lines were extended to 200 miles. Norway soon followed Iceland and eventually the limits became widespread. This resulted in 'quotas' being implemented by some countries, when you could only legally land set amounts of fish in designated areas.

The late 1970s saw many trawlers being laid-up, unable to fish around Iceland and many others being forced to fish for mackerel. But that was another story…

Whilst still waiting for Cordella, I was sent for again by J. Marr and this time asked if I would sail in another small stern trawler, the Zonia, which they had acquired. On this occasion though the ship was in Hull, so I was able to go down to the dock and see it. When I went on board I found it to be quite a neat little ship, it even had a radio room and a cabin for me on the port side of the main deck.

The Zonia was going to Iceland, so this would be my last voyage there. During my twenty-five years at sea, I had spent quite some time in Icelandic waters enduring terrible weather and freezing conditions. So it came as no surprise that my last trip to the area was also marred from the start by bad weather.

When we arrived we were still faced with the same procedure of 'fishing boxes' protected by the Royal Navy. You could leave the boxes providing that you fished outside the new limits laid down by the Iceland authorities but this of course greatly restricted your available fishing grounds. However, the weather remained our greatest hazard, far more than the gunboats. Iceland was notorious for stormy weather but we stuck it out. After a period of fishing and steaming into various positions though, our fuel, freshwater and provisions were getting low. We had to leave Iceland and make for the Faroe fishing grounds, eventually making our way to the South Orkneys.

We were now very low on everything, so we entered Sandvick Bay and went alongside a small pier to take on water and provisions. This was only a small hamlet but there was quite a lot of activity on the other side, as this seemed to be where a terminal for 'North Sea Oil' was situated.

We left the bay and commenced fishing again but later 'under orders' we were bound home, arriving back in Hull at St Andrew's dock.

It was the end of my Cod War adventure and the end of my waiting period. The Cordella would be returning soon. So ended an era. I would not see Iceland again. We had been forcibly driven out from all its fishing grounds. Now it was restrictive fishing only - and quotas!

So the Cordella was on its way home. For the next six years I would be sailing in Cordella apart from two trips, one in Farnella and one in Junella, which I will explain about later.

Meanwhile, until the Cordella arrived, I spent some of the time at college and some with my family, taking my granddaughter for days out and working on the allotment, which still seemed a strange experience compared with sailing the Arctic Ocean. But then as soon as Cordella arrived, it was time to prepare to go to sea again.

I went down to the dock and looked around the whole ship. Everything looked fine. Once aboard I had a word with my relief radio officer who had taken my

Robert Baillie

Junella

place and all seemed to be okay.

After a week in dock we were due to sail. It was time to sign on the log and meet Ron Boughen and all my old sea friends again. These included 1st mate Eddie Fuller, 2nd mate Fred Smith and of course my best friend on board, the cook and a great old bread-maker, Horace Barker, or 'The Colonel' as he was known to everyone who knew him.

As 1974 came to an end I reflected with some concern about the things that had happened, which would effect the future of Hull's fishing industry. I feared that the Icelandic Cod War would not only prove a huge victory for Iceland but also undoubtedly signal the eventual decline of Hull's trawling fleet...

I was going to experience all the new limits and quotas and on board we were going to be deluged with filling in forms about the amount of fish we caught each day, the amounts of fish on board and the positions we had fished. And worse still, we would only be able to fish where the country in question allowed us. Over the next few years gunboat activity would be greater, enforcing the rules. We were certainly going to experience this as we were boarded many times. The other side of the story was that there was going to be a lot of illegal poaching in areas where we shouldn't be, at least when there were no gunboats near...

Sailing on the Cordella in the late 1970s certainly proved eventful. Most of the time we fished the Norwegian coast, the White Sea, Newfoundland and Labrador. But one voyage was away from these areas when we set sail for the Canadian grounds intending to fish there. But information received showed that a number of stern trawlers were already fishing successfully off the American coast in a position at

Robert Baillie

George's Bank.

We had never fished the American coast before but navigating there was no problem with the Loran navigating aid. The only difference was that it was a longer steam to get there but reports were so good that we had to go. Eventually after days of steaming, we arrived and could not believe what we were told on the radio; up to 300 baskets of haddock, but even better than that, up to 15 baskets of prime lobster with it.

We shot our gear immediately. The weather was calm and hot so we towed a short tow and there it was! Our first trawl was full of the best haddock and baskets of lobsters. This was it I thought. We would never be poor again.

While laid processing our catch, I was on watch on the bridge looking over the side and was shocked to see a shark nosing around where our fish offal was being pumped overboard. On hearing about this the boys prepared to catch the shark by baiting a hook with meat and dropping it overboard on the end of a rope. We hooked the shark but it took five of the crew to bring it on board. But it was far too much to handle so they quickly released it and threw it overboard again.

Our 'haddock and lobster goldmine' was also short lived.

On our radar we could see ships approaching and as they drew closer we could see they were US Coastguard vessels. We were boarded, examined and informed that we were under arrest. Apparently we had too much haddock on board and we were fishing too close to a protected lobster area. Messages were then flashed to our owners. Our fishing license it seemed was wrongly worded. Instead of implying we could catch what we liked, it should have stated that only 10% of our voyage could be haddock and we had already landed over 200 tons!

WAITING FOR THE TIDE

Fortunately our dispute with the American Coastguards was settled and we were allowed to carry on fishing but not on George's Bank. We ended up fishing along the Nova Scotia Coast and eventually off South Newfoundland. When we docked after the voyage the main question that was asked was, 'Did we have any lobsters on board?' The answer was a definite yes, we had plenty!

Another incident that I will always remember took place on Good Friday, April 1977. We had just left St John's, Newfoundland after taking fuel and stores on board and steamed to Labrador. Most of the restrictive fishing was in force and poaching had already become part of the fishing game.

If there were no gunboats around you would take a chance of fishing in an area that you were not allowed in but that you knew had plenty of fish, rather than an area that you were supposed to be in but that you knew had very little. Say no more.

Normally we had a good idea where the gunboats were but just after Easter we had a surprise when a helicopter appeared on the horizon. We were fishing on our own and had tracked the gunboats' movements but never expected a helicopter.

Then the Canadian warship Huron came into sight. We were boarded but luckily we were in the right place by the time he arrived. Anyway we were inspected. Our net measurements, the amount of fish we had on board and the positions that we had fished were all checked.

When all was clear I experienced a pleasant little incident of my own. I was in my cabin with one of the Huron's officers. He noticed a photograph of my granddaughter on my desk that she had just had taken at school. He remarked what a lovely photo it was and what a beautiful looking girl she was and how it would make a great 'pin-up'.

I replied that due to this 'special occasion' of being boarded by Huron, he could have a spare that I had to take away with him. So away went my granddaughter on this warship and I often wondered how far the photo travelled around the world. As she disappeared over the horizon it was back to the old cat and mouse game of pirating.

We docked in Hull on Saturday, April 30 after a 70-day voyage. The Cordella was due its yearly survey so we had a month or so at home to look forward to…

On June 12, 1977, Cordella was still in dock on survey when Capt Ron Boughen and I were asked to take part in another type of voyage. It was a trip to the River Thames as a control ship for a huge protest led by numerous small trawlers.

It was to take place opposite the Houses of Parliament and aimed to highlight to our MPs the outrageous behaviour of the Icelandic Government and its disregard of international law.

They were changing the limit lines and wiping out all fishing grounds, and other countries were following suit, resulting in quotas and ridiculous fishing restrictions, such as you could only fish in areas that a country allowed you to. These actions would undoubtedly bring an end to Hull's deep water fishing fleet and would drastically change the lives of all the city's fishermen.

We boarded the Junella and set sail for the Thames. When we arrived there we picked up our pilot and proceeded along the river. As we moved along the Thames we passed a ship scrap yard and there I observed one of my old ships, Kingston Sapphire, being scrapped.

We continued up the Thames to Tower Bridge and

moored next to 'HMS Belfast'. Here a bar was installed on the bridge for the MPs that would come on board. Next, the Junella was bedecked all over with flags. We spent the first night alongside HMS Belfast. I was asked if it was all right for forty Sea Cadets from the Pool of London to come aboard and would I show them around Junella's communication departments. I agreed and they came on board and enjoyed a tour of the vessel.

The next day we prepared for the MPs arrival and also for a flotilla of small ships that were coming to join the protest from various fishing ports on the east and southeast coasts.

The small trawlers came and booked in on Junella and when they had gathered together there was the sudden blast of all our sirens. A number of large white sailcloth notices protesting against the limit lines floated in the breeze. And the crew from Yorkshire TV's 'Calendar'including Grimsby's future MP Mr Austin Mitchell came on board to cover the event.

The ministers were impressed not only with the protest but more so it appeared with our bridge bar. But it didn't make much difference of course, the limits were already ratified and in operation...

Cordella's adventures on the Canadian coast were coming to a close. Thanks to restrictive and quota fishing brought about after the Cod War, we were soon to finish cod fishing and go into the 'new world' of mackerel fishing around the British coast. We sailed for Canada on Friday, June 17, 1977, less than a week after the protest. The weather was fine and the seas were calm, a distinct contrast to what these areas were normally like when we fished them in winter.

We commenced fishing in Labrador in the calm waters and sunshine where our only company were a few small icebergs. The fishing was certainly not heavy

Robert Baillie

but of course restrictive fishing was in force, which meant the areas available to us were very limited.

We fished steadily on into early July. Then one day while watching on the radar, mainly for iceberg movement, I noticed an echo movement travelling a bit faster than icebergs would. I decided to take a closer look at this movement with binoculars and sighted a Canadian gunboat. Sure enough, we were boarded and the usual checks of our papers, nets, voyage on-board and fishing positions were carried out. We were getting used to this. The voyage ended on Friday, August 19 when we docked in Hull.

One incident involving Cordella that I must include took place when we arrived in Canada at the Grand Banks and commenced fishing.

Here, the captain of the large Portuguese vessel 'Antonio Pascal' called us requesting would our radio officer go aboard his vessel as they had been fitted with the navigational and fishing aid, a Decca Plotter but required a demonstration of its use. I agreed to go across to him. He launched a boat and I was picked up and taken to his vessel.

It was a large, fine vessel and on the bridge were a few officers from other Portuguese vessels waiting for the demonstration. So after showing them all about the Decca Plotter, I was invited to stay on board for dinner and what a fine meal it was.

I returned to Cordella with a large bottle of cognac and a similar container of red wine. The rope ladder was lowered so the cognac, the wine and I, in that order, could be taken back on board. But after that success, disaster was to follow.

The next day while laid, after hauling the trawl, we got our variable pitch propeller fouled by rope and wire and ended up helpless. We couldn't move one way or the other. We called to our sister ship, Marbella, to come to our aid. He arrived and towed us to St John's, Newfoundland.

We docked, sent a diver down and he managed to cut the wire and rope free. That night we sailed, but as we were steaming to Labrador the chief engineer came on the bridge and informed us that we were spewing oil from our propeller and would have to go back.

I hurriedly called St John's radio and we made our way back, once again docking at St John's.

On examination it was found our variable pitch propeller was damaged and we would have to go into dry dock. So for three weeks we were in dry dock as our propeller had to come off.

While in dock an American swordfish fishing vessel was towed in and was waiting for the dry dock. His propeller had also come off but had wedged in his rudder. The interesting thing about this vessel was its crew. They were all Vietnam veterans who had pooled their dollars after the war and bought a boat. So as they had no power or means of cooking our captain Alfie Eagle, who had the Cordella for this voyage, invited them on board to dine with us.

The following evening, they brought some cut swordfish steaks over to us, which we had with chips. But boy were those steaks oily! However, we did hear some very interesting yarns from them about their Vietnam experiences…

As the time we spent in dock with Cordella went on, the quota restrictions continued to take their toll on the industry. After the Cod War, as well as the new limits, we also had quotas. Each ship had a quota allocated to it, meaning that if we were fishing on the Norwegian coast we could only fish to what our quota tonnage was. As soon as that expired we went home and probably did not sail again until our new quota commenced.

While waiting we received a request to return to Norway but this time the job included something different, flying instead of sailing.

The stern trawler Farnella was in Harstad and after being away for some time, the skipper and crew were going to be relieved. So captain Ron Boughen, me and the crew of the Cordella were to fly out to Norway and take over the Farnella to go fishing.

On Friday, October 14, 1977 we flew from Leeds to Harstad, but sadly, not without incident. The plane had a piston engine and was propeller driven. The take off was fine but we hadn't been in the air very long before fuel started to spew out from the port engine, splattering the windows. We thought that we may have to divert to Bergen but managed to hold out to Harstad.

We landed and transferred to a waiting bus that took us to the dock where we boarded Farnella, which except for a few differences was more or less the same as Cordella.

We sailed intending to fish from the North Cape to the Russian coast but on November 1, we were chased out of the disputed zone between the Norwegian and the Russian territorial waters by Russian and Norwegian gunboats because our quota had finished. And that was it, we left for home.

Whilst steaming home we received orders to dock in Newcastle and on Friday, November 11 we docked there and boarded a waiting bus to Hull. So this was going to be the future of the Hull fishing fleet, decimated by limit lines, restrictive fishing and quotas. We were apparently now going to divert to something new - fishing for mackerel!

This was definitely a new venture for me. For the last 30 years I had only fished for cod, haddock and plaice all caught with bottom trawl in the stormy, freezing fishing grounds of the Arctic.

Now we were going to fish off the Cornish coast from Start Point to Lands End and as far west as the Isles of Scilly. But not with bottom trawl, we would be using the pelagic trawl.

Mackerel fishing was a game of hunt the mackerel, mark it when found, shoot the gear, tow mostly in minutes not hours through the mark, then haul and there it was - a trawl full of mackerel.

This mackerel was hauled on board and frozen whole into blocks. But then came a difference as these frozen blocks were then packed into cardboard cartons.

When the ship was full, we steamed to Milford Haven in Wales, from where the crew were transported home by bus, while the voyage was unloaded into a refrigeration ship called a 'reefer' and transported to its destination in Britain or abroad.

Then as soon as the Cordella was emptied, refuelled, stored and was ready for sea again, the crew would return by bus and another voyage would commence.

At the end of November we were mackerel fishing off the Cornish coast again after first visiting Milford Haven to take on board 20,000 empty cartons. And December found us off Land's End.

Here we experienced a new and eye-opening type of fishing, a five-minute tow through the mackerel mark that yielded about 1,000 baskets. After only two tows you had to stop as you had enough. The procedure was then was to steam into Mount's Bay in Penzance, anchor and process the fish. When clear, you went out again to search for the 'fish mark'. This mark showed up on our echo sounder as a big black mark. Its depth was recorded and the trawl was lowered to this depth. The trawl opening was observed on the recorder and you could then tow and actually watch the mackerel marks entering your net. And when you had enough you hauled in your net.

In the first week of December we were still fishing for mackerel off the south coast of Cornwall. Two hauls, then it was into Penzance Bay to process the fish.

One amusing incident I recall from while we were anchored in Penzance was that we discovered there was only one anchoring position where we could get a good TV picture. This was on a certain bearing off St Michael's Mount in the bay. So when we had caught our fish and were bound into the bay to process it, if another freezer was heading in at the same time, it ended in a race to get the best position.

Anchoring in the bay had other rewards. We could get the boat to fetch the morning papers or the post for the crew, as although we were only away for a short time, a letter home was always appreciated.

During the early part of December we also witnessed another local disaster, the loss of a small fishing vessel, the Boston Ranger.

We took part in the search for survivors and the tragedy emphasised that you didn't have to be in the Arctic to lose fishing vessels and crewmembers, it could happen anywhere...

In a short time we were full up with mackerel, usually over 20,000 cartons. But achieving this wasn't as easy as it looked. It entailed hauling, shooting trawls, short tows, massive amounts of fish and continuous 24-hour a day factory work.

This non-stop process took place when the mackerel was dropped into the factory, then sorted, put onto endless belts and then filled into block freezers. After a certain time it was taken out again as frozen blocks and put into plastic bags, then into cardboard cartons, through a banding machine where special banding tape secured the cartons. Finally these were transported into a lift, which descended into a frozen hold where they were stored. Remember, there were over 20,000 cartons. It was backbreaking work in a factory that rolled around for most of the time. But once again the fishermen rose to these new challenges, with no moans.

Soon, we were bound for Milford Haven. The ship and the factory had to be scrupulously clean ready for docking. Waiting in Milford would be a refrigeration ship ready to take our voyage but that was the shoremen's job. Also waiting was the crew's bus to take us back to Hull where we would stay until discharge, completely refuelled, stored and back to sea

It was Christmas so our stay would take in the New Year sailing once again sometime in January. This was indeed a change for us, from 8 to 10 week voyages, to just over 14 days.

We still managed to get under our wives' feet but before we knew it, the holiday was over and it was time to board the bus for the journey back to Milford Haven and to the mackerel grounds.

This continued throughout January to March but another disaster was just around the corner. While fishing off the Scilly Isles on Tuesday March 14 we had a calamity when we heard a loud bang from the engine room. One of the engines had blown, rendering us completely out of propulsion. We were now drifting helplessly close to the Scilly Isles coast. I called for assistance and our sister ship Northella came to help us. Meanwhile on the radar, the coast was getting closer and closer.

Northella arrived and fired a rocket with a line, which we picked up. Then a wire was attached to the line and hauled aboard Northella, which enabled him to slowly pull us away from the land.

As Northella had just started fishing, Junella, who had finished, towed us back to Milford Haven where we stayed until the engine was repaired. Once again the bus took the crew back to Hull but for how long that would be, no one knew. It all depended on how quick the repair could be done. But fortunately on April 15, less than a month later, we left Milford Haven with our engine repaired.

We were bound to the Western Isles in North Scotland, to fish off the Hebrides for a new species of fish, to us anyway, blue whiting. This meant fishing in new grounds and in very deep water.

Another chapter of my career was about to begin...

CHAPTER 12
BLUE WHITING?

We commenced fishing off Barra Head in the Hebrides in 220 fathoms. Once again we used pelagic trawling and fished in very deep water to catch this species, the same as for mackerel but we didn't chase a fish mark like we did when mackerel fishing. Each haul would yield quite a catch of blue whiting. When hauled on board the catch went through the same procedure, being frozen into blocks and stowed in the hold. But on Wednesday, April 19 we had a problem with our refrigeration and had to dock in Stornoway and wait for fridge engineers to fly up from Hull. We remained in Stornoway until Saturday, April 22 when the fault had been mended and left once again bound for the West Hebrides.

While fishing up and down the west coast I received a call from Stonehaven Radio asking if I would take part in a 'radio hook' with the GPO at the Bristol Boat Show. This was a test by the GPO with a ship at sea. We agreed to take part and the radio room tuned our transmitter and receiver to the appropriate frequency on the radio telephone via Stonehaven Radio on the east coast of Scotland to link us to the boat show.

From there I was asked some basic questions such as, Who I was? What type of ship I was on? and What were we doing?

The crowd visiting the boat show were listening in to this. The two-way communication was very clear, once again showing how technology had moved on from the old steam days and was still progressing. From the West Hebrides we moved grounds to the Flannan Islands, then to Cape Wrath and finally to Sulisker.

By Wednesday May 10 we had completed the

Robert Baillie

voyage and were bound back to Milford Haven. After discharging we left again on Sunday, May 14 and returned to the Western Isles to again fish for blue whiting. The one thing that was to our advantage, it was fine weather for the whole voyage.

On information received about blue whiting, we made our way to the southeast of the Faroes. On Wednesday May 17, we started fishing there at a position 61.00°N. 07.00°W. and fished there for nearly all the voyage. On Sunday, May 21 we were boarded by inspectors from a Danish gunboat and our net, voyage positions and papers were examined, the usual procedure. We completed this voyage and docked at Milford Haven on Friday, May 30 and after discharge we left Milford, bound for Hull on June 2. Our route home was via the English Channel, docking at Hull at 05.00 on Saturday morning.

So ended our blue whiting venture but we realised that we would not have been fishing for this species at all, or mackerel, if our original cod and haddock grounds had still been available. Once again we had been deprived of our legitimate fishing grounds by yet another spin-off from the Icelandic cod war.

Crews were far longer in dock now, resulting in the reduction of their earnings.

We were only at sea until the quota was exhausted, which wasn't very long, then back in dock until the mackerel season started. It was usually just one voyage now instead of the continuous sea voyages to the Arctic fishing grounds prior to the cod war.

Still, it was nothing new, in my long career with the Hull fishing fleet, the fishermen always seemed to get a raw deal when it came to political settlements regarding limit lines and quotas. But they kept their dignity and fished on regardless. They were without doubt a very rare breed of men.

WAITING FOR THE TIDE

Another period in dock followed until the start of our next voyage. I used the break to catch up with some gardening, painting and other general duties at home. It was very strange to have all this time ashore after years of almost continuous seagoing. But sadly it appeared as though this was unfortunately going to be the future of fishing.

In the middle of July we were informed that the White Fish Authority had hired Cordella for a specified period to carry out a scientific voyage to study a certain species of fish. And on July 18, with a team of marine biological scientists on board and fuelled stored and crewed, we set sail for the Cornish coast via the English Channel. One of the main species we were to investigate was horse mackerel, a fish that the Japanese seemed particularly interested in.

During this venture we were fishing purely as an experimental ship under the White Fish Authority. We fished in many different areas around the British coast, using mainly short tows. And the marine scientists examined all types of fish and logged the positions and the depth of the water where they were caught.

On Thursday July 20 we fished off the Lizard in Cornwall and on the Saturday 22 off the Pembrokeshire coast. The following day we fished in the Celtic Sea in Southern Ireland and on Tuesday July 25 we were off Valencia Island. From there we sailed up the west coast of Ireland and fished off the Mouth of the Shannon, then off the Scilly Isles and finally off Ushant in France.

On Tuesday, August 8 we fished off Start Point, then at a position off the Channel Islands, then back to Penzance in Cornwall. We then returned to the Scilly Isles, the Celtic Sea and finally to Valencia to carry out further tows.

On Monday, August 14 at 14:00 hours we were boarded by an Irish Republic gunboat, 'Le Setanta'. Our

Robert Baillie

papers and voyage were checked and we were asked what we were doing in that location. The following day, outside the Bristol Channel, we had some success landing 1,200 cartons of horse mackerel. And on Friday, August 18 we docked in Milford Haven alongside the Esso terminal for fuel then left for Ullapool in northwest Scotland to pick some crew replacements.

On Sunday, August 20 we arrived in Ullapool and the replacements were brought out to us by boat. We then started fishing again, this time in North Minch. During the next two days we fished off Cape Wrath, Loch Erribol, the Butt of Lewis and the Flannan Islands before returning south through the Minch.

On Thursday, August 24 at 07:00 hours we passed the Isle of Man and then Blackpool, bound into Fleetwood for stores, then resumed fishing off Blackpool. Here, one of our crewmembers sustained a fractured hand and a broken thumb. The Holyhead lifeboat came out to us and took the man ashore and we commenced fishing again.

On Saturday, August 26 we fished off the Bristol Channel and then off South West Pembrokeshire in Wales. But three days later, on Tuesday, August 29 at 22:45 hours we were ordered to go to Milford Haven to tow the Junella to Hull. She had broken down and was waiting there for us. So after completing the scientific voyage we dropped the biologists ashore and on Wednesday August 30 we had the Junella under tow and were proceeding through the English Channel at 7 knots.

This was a hazardous job as it entailed towing a vessel through one of the world's busiest shipping lanes, especially when you got into the Dover area. It was in this area that we nearly had a disastrous accident.

A hovercraft carrying passengers from Calais to Dover was approaching us at high speed. It looked like he was going to go between us, in which case he would have run right into our towing wires. After many signals he altered course and just avoided Junella's stern before carrying on his way. It was just another incident in our eventful life at sea.

On Saturday, September 2 at 09:30 we reached Spurn L.V. Two tugs were there to take over Junella, before we docked on the evening tide. So ended our unusual voyage. The marine scientists had got the information that they had come for and we had enjoyed a cruise around the south and west coasts of the British Isles, from the Scilly Isles in the south to Cape Wrath in the north. And believe it or not, it was fine weather for the entire voyage. But we were now in dock again on standby until our next voyage, which would find us back mackerel fishing in Cornwall.

On Monday, September 18 at 19:30 hours we sailed from Hull for Cornwall via the English Channel and two days later we were off Start Point ready to commence another set of experiments. This time we were testing some new sounding equipment from Kelvin Hughes Limited. The experiment was with a new net transducer for pelagic fishing. The old type transducer was a device connected to the trawl headline enabling you to observe your trawl on a display on the bridge.

The only snag with this device was that to obtain this signal an electronic cable had to be attached to the transducer up to a cable winch, which payed out the cable and hauled it when the trawl was brought in. But if this cable parted during towing you lost the signal.

This new device had no cable. It looked like a cylindrical bomb and in fact this is what its nickname was 'the bomb'. During our stay in dock certain receiver type parabolic aerials were fitted to the ship below around the keel.

179

Robert Baillie

This little bomb like structure transmitted signal that was picked up by the aerial device and passed to the new echo sounder on the bridge. The great advantage was that no cable was needed.

When the tests off Start Point were finished, we moved to the mackerel grounds off Land's End and commenced fishing.

On Monday, September 25 we entered Penzance Bay to pick up a Japanese boffin who was going to experiment with the new sound and 'bomb'.

We moved to the Scilly Isles and commenced fishing, this time using 'the bomb'. I had to laugh at our little Japanese boffin. He was on board for a few days and he shared my cabin and I had made him a shakedown bed on my settee that was just perfect for a man of his size. I showed him this great bed and left him but when I returned later, his bed was untouched and there he was sleeping peacefully in my bunk. I had to position my 16-stone bulk on the small settee but I couldn't help but smile.

It was more or less my duty to look after this gent, but the next mistake I made was when I took him down for his first dinner. I assumed he ate massive meals like me but when I put the first heaped-up plate in front of him he nearly passed out.

On Thursday, September 28 we had to make our way into Penzance to shelter from a full northwest storm. Later the storm abated so we proceeded out again fishing between Land's End and the Scilly Isles.

Just over a week later, on Saturday, October 7 we anchored in St Ives Bay with a full ship and started cleaning the ship prior to docking at Milford Haven. It was during this time that we nearly suffered another disaster that commenced with an easterly gale.

At the time we were initially okay under the lee of St Ives Bay. But during the night the easterly gale swept quickly round to the west resulting in us being open to huge mountainous seas. We then dragged our anchor and the entrance to the bay seemed to be charging towards us. It was then 'all hands on deck'. The anchor was quickly hauled in and it was full astern as swiftly the ship was brought up head to wind and we dodged. Luckily the gale was short-lived and we were then able to get underway and proceed to Milford Haven.

The following day we docked at Milford Haven, where the bus was ready for our journey home. Another voyage was over.

We had now got used to the mackerel fishing and all that it entailed. There would be no more 8 to 10 week voyages in the Arctic. Instead we would be doing short voyages on the southwest coast of Britain and as soon as we had a full ship, we would proceed back to Milford Haven and get the bus home while the ship was discharged into a reefer ship.

The only snag with this was that we were doing less time at sea and more at home, which naturally resulted in greatly reduced earnings.

On Tuesday, October 24 we took the bus back to Milford Haven, boarded Cordella and were once again bound for the Cornish coast.

There were of course obvious differences between mackerel fishing compared to fishing in the Arctic for cod and haddock. On our Arctic voyages, from the moment we left Hull, the skipper received a full picture of the fishing that was taking place in Newfoundland, Labrador and Greenland, the amount of fish being caught and where the biggest fleet of stern fishers were fishing. This was a result of our unique communication and co-operation schedules where the radio officer played a vital part from leaving dock to returning.

Every day at 11.00, 16:00 and 23:00 hours he

received all this information from all round the Arctic in Morse code and after decoding it and entering the results in a schedule book he then passed it to the captain. This was a massive help to the skipper on the outward voyage. Here before him was an up to the hour report of all the fishing that was taking place and with this information he could decide where to go. But when mackerel fishing this information gathering was no longer necessary. It was very easy to get information of where the mackerel mark was as most of the fishing was done round the British coast, so skippers could keep in touch with each other via a VHF radio telephone set on the bridge.

When a mackerel mark was found, you were quickly informed of its position and as each vessel was only going to take a fraction of this mark, there was plenty to go around. Two good hauls were enough for the day, then it was in to Penzance Bay to process the catch. This was the procedure. Someone had to initially find the mark of course but we were all happy to take our turn searching.

The radio officer wasn't idle on these voyages. One of his main tasks was to keep the electronic equipment working. Your 'fish-finder', echo sounder, connected by a cable to the net for instance was a vital piece of equipment. If that went out of action you had to 'stop fishing'.

You could not watch your net on the recorder and had to quickly haul your net in and keep it on board until the echo sounder or the cable was mended. And if that took a long time, a massive amount of mackerel was lost. So now I was not just a radio officer but an electronics officer as well and the college training came in very handy.

We fished off the Scilly Isles, Lizard Point and around the Eddystone Lighthouse and anchored at St

WAITING FOR THE TIDE

George's Island, Looe, due to very bad weather.

We were soon out again fishing off Falmouth, but had to anchor in Mevagissey Bay because of more bad weather. Then out again fishing off Longships Lighthouse at Land's End, and on Thursday, November 9 we were bound for Milford Haven with a full ship and a day later were on the bus bound for home.

On Monday, November 13 at 11:00 hours we left Hull for Milford and the following day left Milford bound for Cornwall in a southerly gale. On November 15 we were dodging a very severe gale off Start Point but then sailed slowly west and commenced fishing off Land's End. Here, there was some very good mackerel fishing and we were soon anchored in Penzance Bay processing.

On Friday, November 17 we were out again and once more fishing off the Scilly Isles. The fishing was very good, then we laid all night off the Scillys processing. We remained in this position until November 23 when we entered Falmouth to pick up our superintendent engineer to go off Start Point to experiment with a grading machine for mackerel.

We returned to Falmouth on Tuesday, November 28 and after another successful voyage of very good mackerel fishing we were bound for Milford Haven, and then the bus home.

On Sunday, December 3 we left Hull by bus for Milford Haven on our last voyage of the year and the following day we sailed for the Cornwall coast. When we arrived at the mackerel fishing grounds we were immediately in a southerly gale, so there was no fishing on the Wednesday. But on the Thursday in a lull we sneaked in one haul then went into Mounts Bay due to an even worse southeast storm.

We were out again on Saturday when one haul produced a very big bag of mackerel, enough for the day, then went back into Penzance Bay, anchored and processed the fish. Out again, one huge haul, then processing fish off Land's End.

We were short of cartons when we left but a consignment had arrived at Milford.

On Monday, December 11 we returned to Milford to pick up approximately 20,000 empty cartons, then left for Cornwall again.

The next day, we were hit by a westerly storm force 11 and slowly dodged our way into Penzance Bay. On Wednesday, the storm abated and we were out fishing off Falmouth area.

On Thursday, after two hauls, we were laid in Mevagissey Bay, processing fish. And on Friday, after only one haul we were anchored in Falmouth Bay processing. And so it went on.

Day after day we would go out again, shoot the trawl over the mackerel mark, then return to the shelter of a bay to process our catch. Most of the days were very similar, only the locations changed. But soon it was the end of the voyage.

On Friday, December 22, we had a full ship and proceeded back to Milford Haven and the bus waiting to take us home. And the next day I was back in Hessle.

It was my wedding anniversary. I'd been married for twenty-eight years. A lot of sea has passed me by in that time so I had a dram to celebrate and another to our latest adventure, mackerel fishing.

1979 would see a complete change to our mackerel venture. We were to move from the Cornish coast to the northwest of Scotland. But before that it was a Merry Christmas and a Happy New Year to our fellow fishermen…

CHAPTER 13
CORNWALL

The start of 1979 saw us still fishing off the Cornish coast. We fished until January 28, then sailed to Milford Haven to get the bus home. But on Friday, February 2 at 16:30 hours, I left Hull again by bus for Milford and only two days later I was back fishing off the Scilly Isles.

On Monday, February 5 we were boarded by a gunboat, 'HMS Subarton' for the usual check of our papers for the voyage etc.

We fished up to the following Monday when we entered Penzance Bay to pick up a film team. They were coming out with us for a few days to film us mackerel fishing.

On Saturday, February 17 we docked at Milford with a full ship and once again went to catch the bus home. But here we hit a problem as the roads from Milford across Wales were blocked by snow, so we had to come home by train. As I travelled back to Yorkshire through the snowbound countryside, my thoughts went back to my days in the Arctic, stuck in the ice, in temperatures of -20° and full storms. Compared to those conditions, this was a comfortable winter.

On Wednesday, February 28 we sailed for the Scilly Isles and fished there for the entire voyage but the trip wasn't without its problems.

On Monday, March 5 we picked up an object over our propeller and had to proceed slowly to Penzance where a frogman came on board. This highly experienced man got rigged in his diving suit and made his way to our stern. Then with the help of a rope and rope ladder he flopped over the edge, made his way down the sloping stern and calmly disappeared into the murky water.

After a few minutes below the water he came up and signalled that the obstruction was now clear. Then, safely back on board, he enjoyed a huge mug of tea and it was thanks all round.

March 10 1979 signalled the end of the mackerel season on the southwest coast so I was homeward bound once more. How long I would be at home nobody knew but we would wait patiently for the new venture on the Scottish coast, whenever it came…

We were now going to fish for mackerel in Scottish waters from the Isle of Skye, then northwards through the Minch to Cape Wrath. These waters were abundant with mackerel but this was seasonal, usually from August to November.

There was going to be a big change in procedure up here. Our old procedure of full ship, then back to Milford Haven and a bus home would change. Here we were going to fish, get a full ship but then proceed to Kyle of Lochalsh, where a reefer would arrive and we would discharge our voyage to him.

One difference was that instead of dockers discharging our catch, our crew were going to do it. This was a lot of extra work for our deck boys, who had just completed the catching and stowage of the voyage and were now going to discharge it, 20,000+ cartons. But as fishermen, they would do it. When discharged we would leave Kyle of Lochalsh and proceed back out to sea, catch another voyage, then back to land to discharge to another reefer.

The third time would see us out for another voyage but after this one we would return to Milford Haven…

So where did we start to look for the mackerel mark? One way was to find out where the Scot's purser vessels were fishing.

What was a purser? In short it was a seine netter, a type of fishing vessel that when the mark was found would simply encircle it with a net. When the net was in position they simply closed the bottom like a purse, drew the net towards them and with a powerful pump, pumped the fish into tanks full of freezing water.

So when we found a group of them we knew that there was mackerel in the area. But while we were fishing on the Cornish coast we had made friends with quite a few Scots skippers mackerel fishing down there, so over the radio we would get quite a bit of useful information from them.

The first position that we fished was off the Point of Stoer, just north of Ullapool. Here was a massive mark of mackerel. Just one short tow through it and we had a huge net full of fish. One more short tow and that was enough for the day.

It was then find a suitable anchoring place and process the fish. It looked easy but it entailed a lot of work. The shooting process of the trawl, the hauling after probably only ten minutes, depending on the density of the mark. Deckhands having to come up from factory duty to take part in this shooting and hauling of the trawl.

The towing time was sometimes so short that there was no point in going back into the factory as hauling time could be on you within a few minutes. And you often ended up with one huge bag on the deck full of mackerel and one already in the factory being processed. Only when the first one had been cleared could the second bag be emptied into the factory. It was 24-hours working here. When enough fish had been processed and the fish space was empty, then it was up anchor and out to The Minch to start all over again.

With this amount of fish we were full up in a short

Robert Baillie

time but we had the weather to contend with. The Minch could be turned into a horrendous sea by very high winds from the Atlantic reaching storm force. With a factory ship we could not afford to be rolling around in heavy seas especially with all those cartons on board, so on a number of occasions we had to head for the nearest shelter.

We fished in The Minch day after day, from Point of Stoer to Loch Ewe and soon we were full. Then it was time to clean the ship and proceed to Kyle of Lochalsh through the Inner Sound, east of the Isle of Skye.

Kyle of Lochalsh was a typical highland community set in beautiful scenery. It boasted a railway station and a small pier, where we moored alongside a reefer ready to discharge our cargo.

The days started at 07.30 when the fish hold was opened and the crew went down into the hold and commenced unloading the cartoons onto the deck. The reefer's crew then loaded the cartons into his holds. This hard, backbreaking work continued until 19.00 with just one break for dinner.

The cartons were meticulously counted on the reefer and on Cordella and at the end of the day the counts would hopefully tally. The holds were then closed until the next morning and the crew were free to go ashore.

The nearest bar was actually on the small railway station and there was another in the centre of Kyle and the main one in the hotel. The work was heavy during the day so the lads would usually go for a drink when they had finished. But as the bars closed pretty early, they were always back on board for a good night's sleep. This procedure continued until we were completely discharged.

This was solely a Marr's project and our partners

at this stage of the venture were Southella, Junella and Northella. Two ships could be in port together, landing their catches into one reefer. Then as soon as we were fully discharged and ready for sea again, we let go and proceeded slowly through the inlet, north through the Inner Sound off the Isle of Skye, then north back to Stoer.

All the way up the Minch we searched for the mackerel mark. There seemed to be plenty of mackerel around but the secret was to get a mark as near as possible to Kyle so that when you were full you had not far to steam back in to discharge it. The one snag that always remained though was the weather. This was our main enemy and could lose us days in fishing time.

While leaving Kyle we got information that several good mackerel marks had been sighted around Loch Snizort on the West Coast of the Isle of Skye. So we made our way around the north tip of Skye, passed Rubha Hunish and commenced fishing outside Loch Snizort.

We picked up a huge mark and prepared for a short tow through it. When we hauled, there it was a huge trawl of mackerel. We sent it down to the factory before one more haul. It produced the same result again but this time we had to leave the bag of fish on deck and start processing.

Anchoring near to the Isle of Skye was a bit dodgy but there were plenty of places where we could find a good lee and shelter from any strengthening winds. After a few hours of processing the factory was clear so we got the second haul of fish off the deck and below to the factory and we were then ready to commence fishing again.

We hoped to get a good few days work, especially with this type of mark around. And we certainly did well around this area, working down to Dunvegan Head

Robert Baillie

then north again across Loch Snizort.

After a week of fishing up and down the Little Minch the mark had gone but we had already got a few thousand cartons on board. We then received information that there were some good mackerel marks south of Point of Stoer, so we steamed there, managing to clear our factory on the way. As we proceeded north we sighted the pursers hard at work. Then, keeping clear of them, we found the mark and shot our trawl. We observed the trawl and the fish mark on our echo sounder and when we had enough fish we hauled in the full net. This was sent straight below to the factory for processing as we shot one more 'for the deck'.

Soon we were informed of the date that a reefer was arriving at Kyle, so we fished until we had a full ship, then proceeded south and back to Kyle of Lochalsh.

It didn't seem a minute since we were in before. We moored up and started discharging. It was the same procedure, empty the ship and then go out again…

We left Kyle of Lochalsh and returned to the Minch. There we searched for the mackerel mark from Loch Snizort to Dunvegan Head but had no success this time. So it was back north again to our successful position at the Point of Stoer.

The Scots' boats were still working as we passed but they seemed a bit close inshore for us, so we shot outside them on quite a reasonable mark. After two hauls we already had enough to process.

We then noticed the Scots boats moving south, so we followed them, knowing that the new positions would definitely produce good results. We did very well, fishing all the way down to a position off Melvaig and then up to Loch Ewe. We soon had a lot of fish in the factory and on deck, so we made our way to anchor near Gruinard Island beside Little Loch Broom to commence processing.

Gruinard Island was a very interesting location. It was used during the Second World War as an experimental base for testing anthrax and from 1942 when the test took place was deemed uninhabitable for nearly fifty years afterwards. From our anchorage we could read the boards warning about this danger and needless to say, we stayed well clear.

There was another Marr's project taking place in Ullapool, namely Klondiking. I will explain more about this later, as in 1980 I came ashore and became very involved in it.

Another unusual event that took place during this voyage was that we were 'topped up' with fish from a Scots' purser. We were ordered in to anchor at Little Loch Broom and the Scots purser would also enter the loch, come alongside us and transfer his catch of mackerel to Cordella.

The names of the two vessels, the amounts transferred and the time and date was then noted and signed by both captains.

We left Loch Broom and started once again fishing the Minch. The mackerel mark got more abundant and we were soon back to 'two hauls enough', anchor and process, then out again.

This went on every 24 hours, until eventually we were full. It was then again time to clean the factory and the ship and set course for Milford.

On our way back we passed the west side of the Isle of Skye, down the Little Minch passing the islands of Tiree and Islay, then through the North Channel passing the Mull of Kintyre and the Mull of Galloway. We then crossed the Irish Sea, passing the Isle of Man then passed Anglesey, across Cardigan Bay to St David's Head and finally across St Brides Bay into Milford Haven. And after discharging into a reefer we

Robert Baillie

returned home.

In November 1979, when I returned to Hull, I saw the devastation that the Cod War had inflicted on the industry. A few days later I was informed that due to the recession in the fishing industry, Redifon, who supplied radio officers to the deep-sea trawlers, were ceasing operations in Hull. This was the Radio Company that employed me and that I had served for over 21 years.

It was not their fault. They were just another casualty from a once great industry.

I was made redundant on November 28 1979. That never to be forgotten date signalled the end of my deepwater fishing days.

So that was it! My only thought was where do I go from here?

Fortunately that question was soon answered. It was to J. Marr, the company that I had sailed with for nearly all the years that Redifon had employed me.

I was informed that in 1980 J. Marr would have some employment for me. And in March 1980 I accepted a job to come ashore and work for J. Marr Seafoods, Klondiking mackerel in Ullapool…

At the start of 1980 and after serving in the Arctic for 32 years, the recession caused by the Icelandic Cod War was about to severely hit all deep-water trawlermen and their future employment.

I had done my last voyage to the Arctic waters and was at home looking to new fields in the industry and waiting for a new assignment. This came in the March when J. Marr sent for me.

I was going to sail on my old ship Cordella but this time on a totally new adventure.

We were not going to fish but were bound to the Baltic to rendezvous off Gdynia in Poland with Polish trawlers. They fished for cod and transferred their catch to us and we processed it. There was no shooting trawls, no fishing and no hauling, we just took the fish on board and processed it.

On March 2, we left the River Humber bound for Poland with captain David Hinchcliffe.

The following day at 08.00 we were at the River Elbe light vessel picking up a pilot, bound for the Kiel Canal in Germany. At 11.30 we started to make our way through the locks of the canal and at 18:00 we arrived in Kiel and then proceeded into the Baltic.

On March 4 at 08.30 we were off the island of Borholm in Denmark where we picked up a spare engine part for Northella, before we steamed east to a point north of Gdynia in Poland. On March 5 at 13.00 we were at a position 30 miles north of Gdynia awaiting the transfer of Polish representatives to us. On March 6 we were off Gdynia, taking fish on board from the Polish fishing firm, Darlowo.

This is how the operation worked; the Polish fishing vessels would catch the fish, all cod, and then call us by radio that they were ready to transfer it.

We then moved to them and with our stern towards them, we payed a large rope down our stern ramp with a float on the end.

The Polish vessel then picked up the rope and connected it to his cod ends, which had been removed from his trawl full of fish. He then put the lot into the sea and we hauled the rope on board and picked up his fish and dropped it into our factory. We retained his cod ends and he would start fishing again after fixing another set to his trawl. We then processed his fish, logged the amount that he had given us and put this on a delivery note for when he returned with more.

This operation went on 24 hours a day. Our operation in the factory was exactly the same as when we caught it. We continued this procedure up to March 14 when very bad weather forced us to proceed to Gdynia to anchor.

A new device that we had on board was a speedboat called 'Searider'that could do up to 40 knots. This was used for transferring personnel, including Polish and Marr's reps, from ship to ship.

We were anchored at Gdynia until March 17 when we proceeded out and commenced operations again as the storm had abated.

On March 21, the fishing was very good but the temperature had fallen below zero.

The following day was far less busy as our catchers had gone into port as it was voting day. But on March 24, the catchers were back out again fishing and they were now catching close to 40 tons per day. We continued taking fish on board for the next few days but on March 30 we hit a snag. Our usual catchers, Darlowo, informed us that they were to cease supplying us with cod. They were going to fish for sprat, so we were left looking for another firm that could supply us with cod. We did not have long before we went home and when we found out that no more catchers were arriving, we decided to return to Hull.

On April 1 at 21:00, we were already at the first lock on the Kiel Canal waiting for it to be flooded. And the following morning at 08:00, we left the last lock and proceeded down the River Elbe and into the North Sea bound for home. And on April 3 at 18:00, we docked at Hull with approximately 600 tons of cod.

I had now finished on Cordella and was at home contemplating my future.

While I was working off Gdynia, I had been asked if I would consider joining J. Marr Seafoods' 'Klondiking' operation, fishing for mackerel and based in Ullapool in northwest Scotland. This was due to start in September 1980 and as the fishing industry was in a serious recession, I accepted the offer.

The new job meant that I would leave the sea and operate ashore but still in the same capacity of radio communications. So from joining the Fleet Air Arm in 1942 until September 1980, I was coming ashore for the first time in 38 years. At the time I couldn't help but think that it all seemed very sad...

Lisa and I in Jedburgh

Robert Baillie

CHAPTER 14
A NEW LIFE ASHORE

At the start of April 1980, I was in the unusual position of looking forward to spending the whole summer at home. My new job ashore was not due to begin for at least another three months so I was going to make the most of the free time. The first thing that I planned to do was to take my family away on a holiday. But first we had the sad passing of my mother in law, Clara White.

Clara, Rita's mother, you will recall had lost her husband George in the 1930s. He was the chief engineer of Loch Ard that left Hull and was never heard of again. The tragedy meant that Clara became yet another one of the hundreds of Hull widows who lost their husbands to the cruel sea.

Now she had also sadly left us, but would be loved and remembered forever by all her family and friends and by me who knew her so well.

We spent the next few months touring around Scotland and visiting all the east-coast resorts from Withernsea to Whitby, the Yorkshire Moors, the Dales and attended most of the various village fetes in the surrounding areas. This was made even more enjoyable by having my granddaughter with me.

I kept thinking that this was what the shoremen enjoyed all the time and it made me look a little strange going on about my holiday as though it was my first. But where it was routine for them, it was my first lengthy spell ashore after thirty-two years sailing the Arctic.

I spent the remaining time waiting for news about my September appointment with J. Marr Seafoods.

It didn't really thrill me coming ashore but owing

to the severe decline in the fishing industry and the fact that I still had nine years before I was due to retire, a job anywhere was acceptable. I was very grateful that J. Marr had employed me so quickly after my redundancy from Redifon, even though it was the end of my deep-water trawling days.

In August 1980 I was sent for by J. Marr to sail in Cordella to the fishing grounds of northwest Scotland. And on August 15 at 09:00 hours we left St Andrews Dock with our Captain, Dick Taylor, bound for Rockall.

This was my first time sailing with Dick Taylor although I knew him well from when he was the Captain in Newingtons, another casualty of the Cod War. We were going to fish Rockall for small haddock, so we steamed on a course north to the Pentland Firth then west to Rockall.

On August 17 we shot our first trawl at a position 56.30°N. 14.30°W. in 117 fathoms and by August 26 we had on board 17,990 cartons of haddock

On the Monday morning at 08.00 we landed a huge haul of 1,000 baskets of small haddock, it was some catch. Eventually we left Rockall with a full ship bound for Milford Haven, where we docked and caught the bus home. It all seemed very familiar.

On September 13, we left again by bus for Milford, this time on a mackerel voyage to Ullapool, North Scotland. But on September 15, while still in Milford, I received a telephone call from J. Marr that I would leave Milford as planned but I was to be relieved on reaching Ullapool

So we sailed and proceeded to the North Minch but on reaching Ullapool I received another message that my relief had not arrived yet, so I was to carry on fishing until he did. We went north on information received and commenced fishing east of Cape Wrath. There was plenty of mackerel and the fishing was good.

Robert Baillie

But when we had about 200 ton board I was informed that my relief had arrived so we returned to Ullapool.

And on September 21 at 11am a boat came out to take me ashore. As I climbed down the rope ladder the crew were waving me goodbye. I looked at them, then at my ship and I waved back. This was it I thought, my final goodbye to the sea.

This was the end of an era…

So there I was on a boat, making my way into the pier at Ullapool. The boatman Harry McRae would play a big part in this final chapter of my working life.

We came alongside the pier, rolled up and I stepped ashore. They took me up to my new abode, a small whitewashed building named 'Myrtle Cottage'.

I entered and looked around. The black beams on the ceiling were typical of the highlands. I looked out of the window at the impressive view of Loch Broom and the distant mountains.

This was going to be my home for the next nine years for the fishing season from September to March.

I put my gear away in the bedroom and went back outside. I was on a street called Argyle Street only thirty yards away from the Argyle Hotel. I thought that if I wanted to meet some locals then the hotel would be the place to do it.

Inside the hotel I gazed around then walked over to the bar where two men were talking. I introduced myself to them and found out that one was the local electrician and the other, a well-known inshore fisherman named Billy McRae.

The hotel owner then came over, shook my hand and introduced himself as Ian Mattison. Now at least I knew three locals. After a pint or two I left to have a look around Ullapool. It was a small fishing and ferry port.

WAITING FOR THE TIDE

The ferry was the Caledonian McBrane Company, which ran from Ullapool to Stornoway on the Western Isles carrying cars and passengers. This was a typical, highland fishing port with four main pubs, The Seaforth Hotel, The Caledonian Hotel, The Argyle Hotel and The Royal Hotel. It also had a few shops including Charlie McDonnell's mini supermarket, John Mcleod's grocery, Templeman's grocery, a post office, a chemist, an ironmonger, a paper shop and the Fisherman's Bethel. All these would play their part in my stay.

I then went to check out J. Marr's base, which was a portacabin situated behind Charlie McDonnell's mini supermarket. Entering, I saw it was vastly different to my old radio room with just one transmitter/receiver, a VHF communication set, two telephones and a large table and some chairs. That was it. But I soon discovered that there was a lot more to J. Marr's pioneering and enterprising 'Klondiking' project, than just this basic set-up.

The Cod War had decimated the deep-sea fishing with its 200-mile limit but also the Eastern Block countries that normally fished around our coasts, could not any more, so hence the introduction of 'Klondiking'.

The system worked like this; The Scottish fishermen would fish for mackerel, whilst factory vessels from the Eastern Block countries such as Russia, Bulgaria, Rumania, Poland and East German would anchor in Ullapool. The Scots' fishermen would then supply them with mackerel.

The mackerel season usually ran from September to March and was controlled by The Ministry of Agriculture and Fisheries. The total tonnage was laid down for the season and when this tonnage was reached the mackerel fishing would stop immediately. At the beginning of the season J. Marr Seafoods agreed a price per ton with the Scottish catchers and then drew up a contract with them. J. Marr Seafoods also negotiated with the Russians for them to supply a number of factory vessels, which were contracted to us and anchored in Annat Bay, Ullapool for the season.

The Scots fishermen, pursers and trawlers then put to sea and fished for mackerel. And as soon as they had enough, they returned to Ullapool where they were directed to a Russian vessel to discharge their catch.

The Russian vessels worked for us, processing and packing the mackerel into cartons, which were later transferred to a reefer and sent to virtually every country that you could think of. On the larger factory vessels it was literally mackerel in at one end and canned mackerel out the other. The whole operation was controlled from our portacabin base and was what you could describe as 'an offshore export market'. In fact the industry became so successful that we were awarded the 'Queens Award for Export' and each one of the staff received a tie with the award logo on it…

My first few days in Ullapool were spent in the portacabin getting acquainted with the procedure of the operation. This mainly involved directing each catcher to its appropriate factory vessel and the general requirements of the catchers, such as stores, fuel etc.

The situation sometimes arose when too many catchers arrived at once and all the Russian vessels were occupied with a supplying catcher. In this case the catcher would be given a number and then come to the pier and wait for his turn. When a factory vessel was clear and required supplying, the catcher who was next in line, would be directed to him.

Another thing that you had to be careful about was when a catcher had opened his tanks, then later called to report that the factory vessel was now full and the catcher still had an amount of mackerel to discharge. You then had to make sure that he was moved quickly to another vessel. If not and he had to wait for a few hours, his fish could go off.

The Klondiking went on 24 hours a day, seven days a week.

After a day or two getting to know the procedure it was time for me to take a watch so I started with an evening watch from 6 to 10pm. From then on, my colleague and close friend Ray Smith and I did the night watches and Jill, a Falmouth lady and the only member of day staff did the day watches.

The Russian factory ships chartered to our company were already anchored in Annat Bay and the Scottish catchers were already out fishing for mackerel in the Minch.

The Russian ships were mostly from Murmansk and had some fancy names including Vasilisen, Victor Kingisepp, Rybatskayaslava, Kronslava, Sebransk, Rhzev and Zaconcase. They worked for us for the next nine years.

The Scottish catchers were mostly from Fraserborough and included Linarolyn, Star Crest, Aquarius, Radiant Way, Coronella, Convalaria, Glen Helen, Steadfast Hope, Quiet Waters, Orcadius Viking, Radiant Star and Sedulous Conquest.

The operation worked like this; A British gunboat with fishery officers on board was anchored at the entrance of Annat Bay to check on all incoming catchers. For instance, if Orcadius Viking was coming in with mackerel he would book in his tonnage and be given a number on arriving at the fishery protection boat. He was then instructed from our base which Russian vessel he was going to.

After an inspection by the fishery officers he made his way to the Russian vessel that would be

Robert Baillie

alerted to be ready for Orcadius Viking to moor alongside him, open his tanks and commence discharging his catch.

Large square metal bins called 'brails' were used to help discharge the catcher and check what tonnage was landed. The 'brails' were on board the factory ships and when the catcher came alongside they were dropped to him. The bottom of the bin had drainage holes and opened to allow the fish to drop out. The bins held a certain capacity measured in metric tons, such as 1 tonne, .8 tonne etc. Each brail was counted on the catcher and the factory ship, so if Vasilisen's brails were 1 ton and Orcadius Viking landed 200 brails, then that was 200 tons landed. A delivery note was made out, one for Marr's base, one for the factory ship and one for the catchers.

There was plenty of mackerel in the Minch so we were prepared for a huge number of catchers entering. If all the factory vessels were taken up then catchers would have to come to the pier and wait for their turn.

The evening wore on, lots of fishing vessels had arrived, the factory space was being quickly taken up and many vessels were going to the pier to wait.

Fishing skippers were coming up to the base to find out what time they would be getting a factory ship. When I came ashore I had a bit of reservation about leaving the sea. But believe me, I was well and truly still with the sea doing this job and of course I was amidst all my own folk, the Scots.

I looked out at the Russian vessels and thought about how times had changed. I had been on Russian convoys in World War II, assisting them. And I had spied on them in the early 1960s during the Cold War. But now they were here working for us and I was to make many friends with the Russian captains and mates during my spell in Ullapool. So ended my first evening watch, finishing at 22:00 hours. It was then off to the cottage for the night.

The next morning I was up early and as I didn't start watch again until 10pm, I had the full day to get to know Ullapool a little better. I met the owners of the cottage, George and Rosanna Ross, who later during my stay were to become my great friends.

Ullapool, normally a quiet, peaceful little port in the Highlands during the months of October to March became a hive of activity, especially around the pier, during the mackerel season. Fish catchers arrived at the pier constantly. Some had discharged and were in for fuel and stores. Some were waiting to discharge into refrigerated trucks that would transport the frozen fish to places throughout Britain or even abroad. And some were in for repairs. It was continuous, 24 hours a day.

The pier at times was chock-a-block, although one part had to be constantly kept clear for the ferry. Here, our harbourmaster, Donny McLeod, did a great job not only handling the pier but also the anchorage for the Eastern Block factory ships and the general flow of incoming and outgoing vessels.

It has to be remembered that Ullapool was also a prominent shellfish port, where there was a fleet of inshore fishing boats going out and bringing their catches back to the pier. I had already met one of the best inshore fishing skippers Billy McRae, who owned his own boat and was one of the top earners.

Another of my new acquaintances was the grocer John McLeod who owned a small shop in Argyle Street. John found himself going from running a quiet grocery business to suddenly having to supply a whole fleet. There was a constant order from the catchers for bread rolls, milk and groceries when they came to the pier after discharge. Not only was John in big demand but so were the shipwrights, the welders, the fuel suppliers, the electronic engineers, everyone in fact, because Ullapool was really buzzing.

Not surprisingly, the hotels also seemed to be exceptionally busy. Whilst another essential service, with a constant and ever-growing demand, was for boats to run in and out to the factory vessels anchored in Annat Bay. This is where Harry McRae who had brought me ashore, would eventually own a large 'sea-taxi' and supply boat service.

So the days went like this.

After I'd done the evening shift, Ray would take over from 22:00 hours to 08.00 hours for three nights. In the morning at 8am I would have the breakfast ready. After breakfast Ray retired for his 'night's sleep' while I washed up and cleaned the cottage before heading along to the Argyle Hotel to meet the locals. Then I did a bit of shopping, mostly for groceries.

The nearest town was Dingwall, 42 miles away and the nearest big town was Inverness, 60 miles away.

As I had been dropped ashore from the Cordella, my car was at home in Hessle so for the time being my shopping was limited to Ullapool. But after a few evening and night shifts I was informed that one of our staff was going home to Hull for the weekend and would take me to Hessle where I could pick up my car.

So on Friday, October 10 I left for Hessle and would return on Sunday, October 12.

As soon as I arrived home I brought my wife up to date on my new shore job.

She smiled and calmly asked, 'You won't be home for tea each night will you?'

It seemed strange, I was arriving home as a shoreman, no longer waiting for a sailing time and the only ice I would see was on the highland roads.

A shoreman's life? I would just have to wait and see what it was like…

CHAPTER 15
KLONDIKING

On Sunday, October 12 we set off again for Ullapool, this time by road, first to York then up the A1 to Scotch Corner. I decided to take the road through my hometown Jedburgh, then to Edinburgh, over the Fourth Road Bridge to Perth, then down the long stretch to Inverness and from there to Ullapool.

This journey took me through the beautiful scenery of the Highlands, passed scores of deer that roamed practically down to the main road, then finally into Ullapool.

As I drove down into the town I could see the loch in the distance, ablaze in a gold and red sunset. And as soon as I arrived at Myrtle Cottage, I parked the car and stood and stared at the surrounding countryside. This was like another world to me, as different from my many years of sailing the Arctic's frozen wastes as I could ever have imagined.

My colleague Ray was on the 18.00 to 22.00 shift as he had filled in all the nights that I'd been away and it was now my turn to do the 22.00 to 08.00 shifts. So after some supper and an hour in the chair it was time for duty. I closed the cottage door and made my way to the portacabin where I found Ray, ready to hand over.

He told me which ships had been served, which factory ships were ready for fish and which catchers were waiting to discharge.

As well as directing the ships we also had to man the telephones that rang continuously. The calls included enquiries about everything from when ships waiting at the pier would get discharged and which ships were due in with fish, to ones from companies in Hull requesting updates about what was happening.

Robert Baillie

Needless to say, the night watch was always very busy.

While on duty in the early hours the door opened and a foreign-looking gent came in. He introduced himself as Enrique and said that he was Spanish but then to my amazement he lifted the handset microphone and in fluent Russian started talking to the factory vessels. Later I found out that he was an important person in this complex operation.

As well as our company operating in Ullapool there were many others including Joint Trawlers, Caley Fisheries, North Minch, Falfish, a number of Irish companies and our partner company, P & J Johnstone from Aberdeen. There were plenty of mackerel and the night watch was very busy. The pier was a hive of activity with constant arrivals and departures of fish wagons and boats landing their catch into huge refrigeration trucks. There were also a number of fishmeal lorries waiting to collect the fish that had been condemned for either being too small or having been left for too long in the open tanks. The boats would come to the pier and land this condemned fish and the trucks took it away and processed it into fishmeal. The fishermen were paid for this fish per tonne but of course at a greatly reduced price.

A few minutes before 7am I had to telephone and alert our staff about the shore sale, of mostly herring, that took place at 8am in the small, inside market.

A large bell was rung on the pier indicating that the sale was about to start and you could see the rush of fish salesmen and buyers as they dashed along the pier.

Inside was a small platform where the salesman from the boat that was currently selling its fish stood, and soon a huge and noisy auction was taking place. At 08.00 it was also time for me to be relieved by the day staff so after passing over the details of the night's work to Jill, including who had been served and who was waiting, I left the base and made my way to the cottage.

On my way I called into McLeod's grocery for some bread and butter, bacon and eggs, and some porridge oats so that I was ready to cook my breakfast. As soon as I arrived at the cottage, it was a pot of tea first, then turn the cooker on and when breakfast was ready I shouted to Ray, 'Come and get it!'

Over breakfast we had a quick yarn about the night's work, then it was time for my bed, at least until 13.00. So, this was shore life?

The days and nights were always busy and went by fairly quickly. There was always plenty of mackerel arriving, the noise of the fishing vessels discharging into the Eastern Block factory vessels anchored off the pier in Loch Broom, the din of the refrigeration trucks being loaded on the pier by pursers and small trawlers. The continuous coming and going of fishing vessels discharging and let's not forget the ferry running from Ullapool to Stornoway in the Hebrides, carrying passengers and cars to and fro from the mainland.

The little port of Ullapool was buzzing with activity but it wasn't all work for me since I had now got my car up in Scotland. So off duty, I had time to explore the highlands.

I visited Inverness, made trips north to Loch Inver and I motored round to Little Loch Broom and viewed the areas where I had been mackerel fishing, including Gruinarde Island where we had anchored many times in Cordella loaded with mackerel. And on more than one occasion I looked out into the Minch and felt a little nostalgic about my fishing days.

With all this sightseeing though, I was able to get quite a good knowledge of the local highlands of Scotland...

There was also plenty of life in the Ullapool

Robert Baillie

hotels and bars, especially at night when most of the fishermen were ashore waiting for their turn to discharge and mingled with the shoremen who worked for the various firms that were involved in this huge enterprise.

I then heard that the fishing in Ullapool would cease in November and we would be transferring the full operation to Falmouth in Cornwall. This included the Eastern Block fleet and the Scottish fishing fleet, everything in fact.

My next night's operation was particularly hectic.

There were always little incidents happening during my nightwatches and a very funny one that I always remember involved my friend the Spanish gent, Enrique. He was a very important businessman operating with the Russians and had to be out in Annat Bay and make regular visits to the Russian ships.

On this occasion Enrique and his Spanish partner took the Searider and made their way out into the bay to board one of the large Russian vessels.

The normal procedure was to keep in touch with our base when boarding and leaving a vessel and after a few minutes the Russian vessel called me to say that they were safely on board. Then, an hour or so and a few vodkas later, I was informed that they were leaving the Russian ship and returning to Ullapool. But after quite some time had elapsed there was no sign of them coming towards the pier.

I checked with the Russian ship, and yes, they confirmed that Enrique and his partner had left. Then on another radio channel I heard the Fishery Protection vessel anchored at the entrance of Annat Bay calling me. I answered and to my surprise was informed that they had two foreign gentlemen on their bridge, claiming that they were from our base.

This of course turned out to be our two missing

Spanish gents. They had apparently left the Russian boat but had gone the wrong way and proceeded out of the bay instead of into it. They had then sighted the gunboat's lights, moored up to him and climbed a rope ladder before appearing on the bridge.

Their safe return was on board a Scots purser coming to the pier and towing the Searider astern of them. I welcomed them back to base with a huge grin on my face then sat and listened as they tried in vain to explain what had happened.

The operation went on and on and at the end of October we started to prepare to move the whole fleet to Falmouth. Then on Tuesday, November 4 I left Ullapool for Hessle and following a short stay at home left for Falmouth on Monday, November 10…

Travelling along the motorways, the M62, M6 and M5 and eventually across Bodmin Moor my thoughts took me back to my sailing days. Here was a different world. Instead of the big iron ships, the pack ice, the endless storms and -30° temperatures, I was motoring along roads where the weather was quite mild. When I fancied a meal, I simply stopped and had one. Really, this shoreman's life was a doddle.

I drove into Falmouth and went straight to the Royal Duchy Hotel, which was to be our new base. A top room in the hotel had been taken over and fitted out as a communications centre for the operation similar to that in Ullapool. As I stepped out of the car, I gazed over the sea off Falmouth reminding myself again of my Cordella fishing days. When we started fishing these waters from Start Point to Land's End for mackerel, I would have the advantage of knowing these waters and land positions from my time operating with the fleet.

I entered the hotel and made my way up to our new base. The time was around 19:00 and my partner

Robert Baillie

Ray Smith was already on watch. It was then that I realised I would be on nightshift. I enquired where my living quarters where and was informed they were not in the hotel but in some luxurious flats nearby called the 'Anchorage' flats.

Ray and I were going to share the flat, so after procuring a key and some directions, I got in my car and set off to view my new quarters.

As soon as I entered the flat I was very impressed with what I saw. The flat was laid out and furnished very well with all the modern amenities that you could imagine, including brand new cooking facilities and even a breakfast bar. It all looked fine to me.

I was going on watch at 22:00 so I had a short sleep in an easy chair, then made my way back to the base. Of course this was more comfortable than the portacabin, so taking over from Ray I commenced my first nightwatch in Falmouth.

As well as running fishing vessels from our firm we also ran other firm's boats, making it quite a full night's work. The Eastern Block factory vessels were there in position and the mackerel fishing was already very heavy. It followed the usual procedure where the fishing vessel arrived, called base to tell us what tonnage they had on board and then was directed to a waiting Russian vessel for discharge. If a situation occurred when all the Russian vessels were taken up, the fishing vessels would be allocated a number and come to the pier to wait their turn to land their catch.

Now of course we were in a much larger place than Ullapool and more drinking places were available alongside the pier for the waiting crews. And being true seafaring men it was usual 'harbour nights'.

The night wore on and around 07.00 hours the telephone calls from the firms that we were handling increased even more. What was the situation with their vessels? Who had landed? Who was waiting and what time would they commence landing?

There were also calls from the Russian factory ships informing us that they were ready for the next fishing vessels. These were welcome calls as we then contacted the next boats that were waiting to discharge.

At 08.00 my day relief came in. I handed over to him and made my way back to my quarters, stopping at a small grocery store for the usual bacon, eggs, bread and butter. I wasn't sure what the provisions were like so it was safer to take some along. I entered the flat and put the kettle on for a cup of tea, then got out the frying pan for the bacon and eggs. Next I tapped on my colleague's door and shouted, 'Wakey, wakey!'

Then, while the bacon was sizzling and over a mug of tea we discussed the night's operation.

Christmas was now approaching and the operation would close down over the Christmas and New Year period. As the Christmas week drew nearer, most of the Russian vessels and the Scots' boats started to leave. They would return after the New Year for the remainder of the operation. Only a few of the larger factory vessels and a few of the Scots' catchers remained.

I was informed that the Scots' personnel at the base would remain over Christmas and go home for the New Year. The Scottish members of the team included David Middleton from our Northeast Scotland Management, Harry McRae and his support boatman from Ullapool - both down for supplying and ferrying duties to and from the Russian vessels - and myself to look after the communications. As there were still a number of refrigeration ships taking cargo from the factory vessels, so there was still plenty of work to be done.

Robert Baillie

I telephoned my wife and informed her that I would be coming home for New Year. Then, before I knew it Christmas Day had arrived.

I enjoyed a lovely Christmas dinner at David's place, a flat on Falmouth pier. David's wife had come through for the holiday so the cooking of the turkey was in good hands.

On the day we met in the flat, where the table was ready, and after pre-dinner drinks we were joined by the Spanish rep, Enrique and his wife Rosa, who were prepared to fly out to Spain later in that evening.

Ray and I continued to man the base for the rest of the week, then on Tuesday, December 30 I set off for home to spend the New Year with my family.

This seemed like a strange life to me after all the years that I had spent at sea and when if I had celebrated New Year at home, it had been only by chance that I was in port at the time...

I spent a wonderful New Year at home but all too soon on January 5 1981, I was bound back to Falmouth. When I got there the operation was already in full swing again with huge amounts of mackerel being caught. The Russian factory vessels were also back and ready for action. The Scots fishing vessels brought in their full catches of mackerel and landed them on the Russian vessels before going straight back out to sea again. Some of Marr's smaller vessels based in Fleetwood were now also taking part in the procedure that went on 24 hours a day.

Once again Falmouth pier was alive with catchers waiting to land, catchers who had already landed and others coming in for suppliers and fuel. There were also more and more refrigeration and fishmeal trucks arriving and this all had to be organised and directed from the base.

WAITING FOR THE TIDE

Sunday, March 1 brought the mackerel season on the southwest coast to an end. So it was time to clear all existing vessels of their fish and prepare the Russian vessels for departure. We then had to load up all the gear from the hotel that had been used during the season's fishing operation to transport it back to Hull. And by Saturday, March 7 I was on my way home. So ended my introduction to Klondiking…

Back in Hessle I had a long holiday to look forward to as I wasn't due back in Ullapool until August. This was going to be the longest time at home that I'd known, over five months. But what do you do as a 'shoreman' with all that time on your hands?

'Get in the swing,' they told me.

'You do the gardening, you prepare for your holidays, you even do regular shopping at weekends,' were other suggestions.

Well, okay, here I go, I thought.

After thirty-three years of continuous sailing, I was actually going to be a landlubber.

No, I wasn't thrilled at the prospect. I knew that it was going to be great to be with my family but my main thought was, could I actually stick the shore life?

Time would tell. And it was a wonderful feeling to be at home to enjoy such an experience...

March and April found me in a new mode of life. Until August I was free to do anything I liked. There was no sailing, no stormy seas, no Arctic -20 to -30° temperatures and no pack ice!

But what should I do?

The first thing was a bit of gardening, then some outside painting. I thought that a few days of this and I may get into the shoreman's way of life. So plod on.

I worked around my property until the middle of

213

Robert Baillie

May but there was not much adventure doing that so I decided that a little tour of Scotland would be more exciting. So on Saturday, May 9 the car was packed and fuelled and with Rita and our granddaughter Lisa, we were off.

The first place I visited was the cottage in Jedburgh where I was born. It was my first time back for 40 years. I had left during World War II to join the Fleet Air Arm, flying as a Telegraphist-Air gunner.

For a fortnight we travelled around the borders of Scotland. The weather was very hot and we all had a great time up there. And I finally returned to the place where I was born on Saturday, May 23. From then until August was solely taken up with travelling around the Yorkshire Moors and the Yorkshire coast.

To me starting this new career had been like starting a different life. And all this seemed like a new world…

The call came for me to pack and make my way to Ullapool and on Friday, August 28 I was back in Myrtle Cottage and preparing for another season Klondiking. The Russians were anchored in Annat Bay alongside other Eastern European factory ships. The fishing season would last until November then we would move down to Falmouth again. Once more, massive amounts of mackerel were caught and discharged to the Russians. And after another successful season, in November all the Russian fleets and most of the personnel from our base moved to Falmouth but I was informed that I was not going with them. I was to go with David Middleton to Mallaig in west Scotland…

On Sunday, November 15, after studying my map, I left my cottage and made my way to Loch Ness, then to Fort William and from there to Mallaig. I arrived in Mallaig about teatime. I had never been there before but

WAITING FOR THE TIDE

I spied two ladies and pulling up to them said, 'I take it that I am in Mallaig, could you direct me to the dock?'

They pointed in a direction to the right and then asked, 'Are you from Marr's?'

'Yes,' I answered, 'You could say I'm the advance guard from Marr's.'

Then making my way to the small dock, I hung around for a few minutes, until David appeared.

'Come on boys, we'll go for something to eat, then to our living quarters,' he said. So over a meal in this hotel I got my first briefing of what we were going to do. First of all, this was herring fishing and David was the manager, his first command.

I would set up a base and in company with P & J Johnstone, Alisdair Murray and Derrick Bond, would run the project.

Then a Russian factory ship would anchor in Loch Nevis and prepare to take herring. And some of the Scots' catchers that had not gone immediately to Falmouth would fish for herring and bring their catch in to discharge to the Russians.

David showed me the way to our quarters. It was definitely not a small dwelling. This was Irving House situated on a hill overlooking the Isle of Skye.

Inside was sumptuous, laid out with a sitting room with very large windows where I could sit and look at the entrance to Mallaig, the Isle of Skye, the Isle of Rhum and the Isle of Eigg. So this was it, we were now waiting for our first lot of herring.

The base was set up in an office immediately above the indoor fish markets. Inside I had the usual radio communications set, telephones and telex set. I was now standing by for the first boat in...

Robert Baillie

The Russian factory ship, Victor Kingisepp

CHAPTER 16
MALLAIG

So there I was in Mallaig, another of the West Coast fishing ports. It was Sunday, November 15, 1981 and the weather was just what I was used to, thick snow and minus temperatures.

Mallaig was a small community with a few shops including a grocer's, a butcher's and a little supermarket, centred round a small square. It was also a very active fishing port, fetching in all species of fish.

Nearly all the male population were either fishermen or employed on the bustling fish dock.

The huge fish office building and indoor fish market was going to be the centre of our activity until the end of December. Whilst Irving House, situated on Coteachan Hill would be our home for the duration of the operation.

One of the first things we had to sort out was the eating arrangements of the four operational men.

I volunteered to do the one main meal of the day, which would take place at 6pm each night. And we decided that each of us would put £15 in the tin to buy the ingredients.

I would look after the night duty, the herring usually arriving around three in the morning. I would be there until around 11am, then make a trip to the small supermarket, followed by the butcher's and put my order in. Then I'd go the Centre Bar for a pint and a dram, and a yarn or two with the local fishermen, before returning to get my meat from the butcher's and collect my groceries and proceed to Irving House for a short sleep. Finally, I would then get the evening meal ready before informing the boys who were on the fish dock to, 'Come and get it!'

Robert Baillie

They would arrive and the meal would be dished up. It was then time for me to go on the dock to our base and listen out for the fishing boats' times of arrival, which was mostly in the early hours of the morning. So this was the procedure to the end of operation.

Meanwhile the large Russian factory vessel was now anchored in Loch Nevis with the fine name of 'Matochkin Shar'.

We would then get the information that the first fishing vessel was arriving and he would come to the pier. A sample of his catch was brought up into the fish market, examined and passed and then he would be instructed to move to the Russian vessel, which had been alerted and was ready to take his catch.

These large Russians were able to take two fishing vessels, one port side, one starboard side, landing both together. When the vessels had discharged, delivery notes were exchanged, one for base, one for catcher and one for the factory vessel, then they were off to sea again to catch more fish. This went on each day but then what happened was that where we all thought it would be just a small operation developed into a very large one.

More catchers heard how successful the herring operation was and came to take part. We then had a huge amount of herring arriving, so much so that we had to call our headquarters in Hull to send more factory vessels and also more staff. This is when my good friend, radio officer Ray Smith was sent up to Mallaig from the Falmouth operation.

He was due to arrive on the Glasgow to Mallaig train so I went to the small station to meet him.

When the train pulled in, 'Smithy' who was unfortunately at the back emerged and seemed to step straight out into a snowdrift.

'Welcome to Mallaig Smithy,' I shouted. I

grabbed his case and we proceeded to the Centre Bar. Then, refuelled and ready to go, we walked up the hill, again knee deep in snow and into Irving House.

I took him to the big window and said, 'See that scenery Smithy.'

He looked at me and replied with a sickly grin, 'Yes, I have just ploughed through it.'

It was great to have him back.

Saturday night was dance night, this was the night of the week. So we dressed up and went down to the hall. It wasn't, 'Could I bring a bottle of whiskey in?' More like, you were not allowed in unless you had one!

When we entered the dance hall the Master of Ceremonies shouted through his microphone, 'Ladies and gentlemen, welcome to the men from Marr's.'

It turned out to be a great night. And fortunately, Sunday was going to be a quiet day, so we could all get a good sleep...

The time passed quite quickly and soon the end of the operation, December 21, was in sight.

Mallaig was still under a blanket of heavy snow and the freezing temperatures continued to drop even lower. The snow was that thick that coming out of Irving House I could not find my car. I had left it at the bottom of the hill and it was completely covered by several foot of snow and required serious bit of 'digging out'.

That was just one of the many incidents caused by the severe Scottish winter during our stay.

And another one that I'll never forget happened following a very heavy night's snowfall.

When the snow had stopped, I cleared the path at the back of Irving House, then left the back door open whilst I went indoors for something.

While inside the house I heard a movement near

the back door and went to investigate. To my amazement, standing in the doorway was a very large ram. Now sheep wandered all over the streets and beyond in Mallaig but it was the first time I'd found myself face to face with a ram. I went up to it, got hold of its horns and attempted to force it back out. But it didn't appreciate that and the situation quickly turned into a wrestling bout, me versus the ram. Fortunately, I slowly managed to force it backwards and out of the door where it turned quickly and disappeared into the whiteness.

A few days later I suffered another mishap that was caused by the freezing temperatures rather than the snowfall. One very cold morning I had just done my washing and hung it out on the line before going down to the dock on duty. When I returned in the afternoon there was the washing standing to attention, frozen solid. I didn't need a basket to bring it back into the house. I just took it off the line and marched it in…

So the days went on with plenty of herring coming into the small market. And when a sample had been passed, the catch was then taken out to the Russians in Loch Nevis.

Before long, the closing date was approaching fast. The Scots fishermen brought in their final catches and the Russians prepared to finish and leave.

It had been another very successful operation and at 10am on Wednesday, December 23, my wedding anniversary, Ray and I departed Mallaig and set off for home. But little did we know that the trip would unfortunately turn into a journey to end all journeys.

Ray didn't drive so it was all left to me.

'Slow ahead', it was snowing heavily and with a slight frost, so the first part of the journey along the road to Fort William seemed endless but eventually we arrived. Then taking the A82 we proceeded south. By the time we got to Glencoe I was going along at five miles an hour and couldn't see the road for the snow. And when we reached Bridge of Orchy it was touch and go whether we could carry on. The snow was very heavy and the windscreen wipers were freezing up. So we had to stop at regular intervals and clear the frost and snow off.

After a period of slithering and sliding we reached Loch Lomond. We then skirted around Glasgow and proceeded to Carlisle, Penrith and on to Scotch Corner. When we finally arrived there, it looked like a disaster area. Despite the snow it seemed very dark with a large number of cars just left abandoned by the roadside. A policeman asked where we were going and when we replied to Hull, he looked at us in a way that suggested he doubted whether we would make it. But here is where my great Arctic experience came in.

I thought that as we had come all this way, there was no way that we were giving up. The conditions didn't bother us and as long as the car kept going we were continuing on our journey.

So down the A1 to York and the last part of the journey, the road to Hull. It was still thick snow but there was less frost, so 'half ahead' and eventually we arrived in Hessle just after midnight. We stopped at our house and Ray came in for a dram before deciding to get a taxi to Hull. So ended my anniversary day.

I thought to myself I must have been born to float around on ice and snow. But now it was time to celebrate Christmas 1981 and the New Year before moving to Falmouth in Cornwall for another mackerel season. This would take us up to March, then spring and summer at home before returning to Ullapool in September 1982 for the start of the next mackerel season.

Robert Baillie

After Christmas and the New Year at home we returned to Falmouth. This time though we were in a new base in the Falmouth Hotel where some rooms right at the top of the hotel had been fitted out for operations. This meant rigging up aerials on the roof and communication sets in the rooms.

Once again the Russians and other Eastern Block ships were anchored off Falmouth and ready to take mackerel. The Scots fishermen and others had arrived and were already fishing.

I picked up Ray in Hull and drove to Falmouth. On arriving we sorted out our new quarters, which were flats next to the Falmouth Hotel that were joined to the main building. They were very comfortable with self-catering facilities available or we could eat in the main hotel if we wished. And to me, after a life in the Arctic where you had to make do with what you had on board your vessel, this was what I would call 'a life of luxury'.

We didn't need to go outside this complex. We had bars, restaurants, a swimming pool, a dance hall and after 11 at night we could watch films in our quarters via our TV. I was probably getting the wrong idea about shore life.

We would be there from January to March, with watches 24 hours a day. Ray Smith and I worked continuously on the evening and night watches.

Heavy mackerel fishing resulted in the non-stop arrival of full fishing vessels, some discharging to the Russians and some waiting a turn at the pier. The only time it stopped was during very bad weather.

Here I must mention the fishing vessels and their skippers whom I would be dealing with in my new career in this Klondiking venture. These vessels were the backbone of our operation and without them the project could never have taken off.

The season was soon fully underway and the

weeks passed quickly. It seemed no time at all before it was the end of February and the operation was due to finish in March. So it was time to finish fishing, prepare the Russian vessels for departure and stow all the gear into the hired transport, ready for the trip back to Hull.

Smithy and I departed Falmouth bound for Hull where we would be at home for the whole summer until August when we would once again be back in Ullapool to start another season.

My summer at home was spent gardening and taking the family away on trips to the seaside and the North Yorkshire Moors. We practically lived on the moors spending quite a bit of time in the fishing port of Whitby and the moors' village of Goathland. This of course was a new world to me. I had a full summer free to go where I wanted. But not on a holiday abroad. We did not fancy careering around foreign beaches. After all, we had plenty to explore on the British Isles. We usually spent our holidays in Scotland but by the time came for my departure back to Ullapool, we had certainly seen a lot of Yorkshire. There was nothing like carrying your own stove and picnic supplies and getting to some remote part of the country, but not too far from a fish and chip shop. The shoremen may have wondered why I was so enthusiastic about all this but they had not spent thirty years in the Arctic...

In September 1982 we returned to Ullapool for the mackerel season. The Russian and Eastern Block ships were anchored and preparing to receive the first catches and the Scots fishermen were already out at sea. As well as the Scots we had the Glen Rushen and Glen Helen from Fleetwood and newcomers Boston Halifax and Boston Stirling from the southeast coast. The Russian vessels included Kronslava, Karpagory and Rudina, the Bulgarians; Glarus, Fizalea and Kondor, the

Robert Baillie

Poles; Morag and Wigry and the East Germans; Junge Veldt and Granitz. These were some of the names that we would get to know during this complex operation.

My good friends the Spaniards, Enrique and Felix, were essential to this project as they both spoke Russian fluently.

So it was back to business. In came the Scottish fishing boats loaded with mackerel. They booked into the fishery office and we directed them to a waiting Russian vessel to discharge. Then they were back out to sea. On and on, night and day, some catchers selling to buyers on the pier. Refrigeration trucks loading their catch and heading off south. Some mackerel unfit for selling being loaded into fishmeal trucks. Fishing vessels calling for fuel, calling for food, supplies, water etc. Fishing vessels calling for repairs, even calling for a diver to attend to an obstruction round their propeller. Fishing vessels calling for buses to take the skipper and the crew home. And of course fishing vessels at the pier waiting to discharge to the Russians, calling to find out what time they would be discharging. The base telephones ringing constantly with calls from Hull for progress reports, calls with new orders and calls from firms who have surplus fish, asking if there is any space for them on our Russian ships. And of course, calls from ships on the fishing grounds, giving their ETAs. All this was being handled in our base, 24 hours a day.

This operation was going to make quite a few people very rich in Ullapool. This huge complex operation needed ship Chandlers, supplies of food, fuel, welders, shipwrights, boatman to run a service to the ships, and a taxi service to make continuous runs to Inverness, the railway stations and the airports.

The once quiet Ullapool was now a hive of activity. One of our main requirements was a boat service from the pier to Annat Bay, to serving the ever growing workforce. Here my good friend and boatman, Harry McRae, who brought me ashore from Cordella, was steadily setting up a service in collusion with our firm. He had mustered a few boatman and even now had a portacabin headquarters at the foot of McBrayne's lorry park. Harry would eventually become the head of a large boat service, 'Sea Taxis'.

My good friend, John McLoud, who owned the small grocery shop was also eventually going to be 'big time'. Instead of supplying a few groceries to the local population, he would be delivering truckloads of provisions to the Eastern Fleet and the Scots fishermen. Initially however, he faced competition from supermarket boss, Charlie MacDonald, who also had an eye on this provisions' service.

The next thing that we had to do was to arrange accommodation for the operators of this vast and expanding business. We contacted the owners of holiday accommodation, houses and flats who might be interested in earning a winter income, renting out their properties to the firms involved in this complex Klondiking operation.

So it went on, with Ray and I running the nightshifts in the base and the day watch teken care of by the management and Jill, a unique lady who was quite acquainted with the seafaring world having spent quite some time sailing in her father's boat out of Falmouth.

We must not forget the pubs and hotels etc. They were having a merry time. As the world knows seafarers like the odd dram or two and Ullapool was full of them when the boats were at the pier. So the once quiet fishing port was alive and jingling.

We operated up to December with very heavy mackerel supplies coming in from the Minch up to Skye. We were working day and night supplying the

Robert Baillie

Russians, East Germans Bulgarians and Poles, and once again the pier was a hive of activity. It was strange to see the Russians coming ashore to do their shopping. What we took as everyday commodities to them appeared to be luxuries. They shopped around in groups and were a very disciplined crowd, mainly shopping for coffee and chocolate.

Over the next few years I made many friends with the Russians, Poles, Bulgarians, East Germans and Romanians during our operations in Ullapool.

Port activities were not always continuous. We had the effects of bad weather to deal with that affected both the fishing at sea and also the Russians at anchor in the bay and off the pier. Ullapool and the offshore grounds were frequently subject to continuous low-pressure areas coming in from the Atlantic resulted in severe storms and gales in the region of 90 mph. Of course this stopped fishing operations and if this weather was of a prolonged nature and lasted for more than a few days, then you had fishing vessels coming in and anchoring and the crews going home until it was clear again. This was another job for the base, ordering buses to be on the pier when the fishermen came in. One great danger was their boats laid at anchor off the pier with no one on board. We always kept a continuous watch on them in case they moved. A bigger problem was the large Russian vessels outside in Annat Bay. During the storms, if they dragged anchor they didn't have much room for manoeuvre, so one of our main duties was to be kept updated from the Met. stations about weather situations. Believe me, we experienced some rude storms up there.

One amusing incident occurred when two of our staff went out in the 'Z' boat to collect some delivery notes from the Russians. While returning an increasing wind drove them onto the shore. While I was on night watch, my telephone rang and to my surprise it was one of the lads. His first words were, and I quote, 'We have a distress!'

'Where are you calling from?' I asked. And he replied, 'A telephone kiosk.'

Good Lord I thought, how can you be in distress and calling from a telephone kiosk?

The story was that they had been blown ashore, luckily enough at the very place where a telephone box was situated. We soon had help to them and a few minutes later two bedraggled personnel entered the base. It was then essential that two-way radio sets would be compulsory when proceeding out in the 'Z' boats. You had to check with base when you left the pier and again as you left the ship in Annat Bay. The next thing that was suggested was to have wet suits available and somewhere to dry them after use. The men going out in those bouncing boats were continually wet and after climbing rope ladders to board and then leave various ships, it was a very damp experience. But the operation carried on regardless. These difficulties were part of the job and of course the fishermen at sea were going through plenty of far worse conditions to bring the mackerel in. I should know, I had 33 years with the Hull fishing fleet and a few years' mackerel fishing around the British coast.

So that was it. The season had been going since September and was now coming to an end. The usual procedures were started to get the fishermen and their boats cleared and away home. And the Eastern Block ships finished and back to their homelands.

As for us, we packed up our gear once more, and there was the usual farewell party as another season drew to a close. Then it was home for Christmas and the New Year…

CHAPTER 17
FALMOUTH

At the beginning of January 1983 we were ordered to Falmouth but this season was going to be very different for me. Rita was normally left on her own at home whilst I was away and I came home once a month from Thursday until Monday.

On this occasion however, I was informed that I could take her with me to Falmouth for the season, which would end in March and that accommodation had been arranged for us in the Falmouth Hotel. This was great news, so on Monday January 3 we arranged for our house to be looked after by our neighbour and the following day Rita and I drove to Falmouth.

This was certainly a new venture for us. We arrived at the hotel reception at around 6pm and collected the keys to our flat that was in an annex connected to the hotel. Then we got our luggage and provisions from the car and entered our luxurious new home. After we got settled in, we made our way into the hotel to find the rest of the operation's staff. There they were in the main lounge bar. Rita and I reported our arrival and all was okay, especially as I didn't have to be on watch until the following day. So we returned to the flat, had a bit of supper and then retired, ready for an early start the next day.

On Wednesday I reported to my new base that was situated on the top floor of the hotel. As the season was just commencing a day watch was set up. I would work during the day and later on, when the operation was underway, I would revert back to my usual night watch.

The Eastern Block ships were arriving with a number of Bulgarian, Russian and Eastern German vessels getting into position and anchoring in Falmouth Bay.

The Scots were also on their way and some already actually fishing. We also had a new team of catchers, the southern Irish, with names like Antarctic, Atlanteen, Paula, Sheanne, Albacore and Neptune. I also spotted the Hull vessel, Peter Scott.

The mackerel started coming in and with the Scottish, Fleetwood, Boston and Irish vessels, it was certainly going to be heavy. Ray and I then started the usual night watches of three nights 22.00 – 08.00, then three nights 17.00 to 22.00 - every day including Saturday and Sunday. And I soon found that there was the benefit of working the night shift.

I would come off at 8am and return to the flat where Rita had breakfast ready. I then retired until around 1pm while Rita did her shopping, then I'd be up again, dressed and ready for off.

I decided that while Rita was there I would take her all over Cornwall. So our first day out was to Lands End, then Penzance where we indulged in their fine fish and chips in a splendid little restaurant. During the season we would be a frequent visitors there. After our meal it was back to the 'hotel' for a quiet hour's TV before going back on night watch. This seemed more like a holiday to me especially as it was all expenses paid.

So back to base and a word with Ray as he passed the watch over to me. The phones were ringing, ship's skippers were shouting out on the radio and my Spanish friend Enrique was talking away in Russian to some vessel's captain. This was the scene on a normal night watch.

Then some Scot's skippers, Irish skippers, even English skippers would enter, wanting to know their turn number. A little argument could easily break out as to why one was getting preference over the other. This often happened when trawler and purser captains were in together, with trawlers being given preference, as they could not keep their catch for as long as pursers.

The purser's skipper would often feel aggrieved if he had been waiting many hours to get discharged only to find a trawler had come in and had to be discharged first. And he could get particularly irate if a trawler had landed its catch, gone back out to sea, sighted a fish mark outside Falmouth and was back in again with fish demanding priority.

But this was Kondiking at its best. Look out!

This would be our last season in Falmouth as the southwest coast was going to be closed for mackerel fishing. All future seasons would be at Ullapool. So as well as my watch keeping and operating the complex Klondiking, I was going to take Rita to see as many of the lovely resorts on the Cornwall coast as I could. So each time I was on night watch, I was ready at 13:00 hours to take Rita on a visit to a different place.

After Penzance we visited St Ives and whilst in our favourite fish and chip shop I recalled my experience when I was on Cordella and we dragged anchor outside St Ives' harbour in a westerly storm.

The owner of the chip shop also remembered the night when it happened.

'I thought you were going to crash into our harbour,' he said.

'Yes, it was a near thing,' I replied.

We spent another hour or two in St Ives before returning for my night shift. The following day our next visit was to Newquay. We also made trips to numerous other places including Redruth, St Austell and Truro. Most of our time though was spent in our favourite haunt, Penzance. This was undoubtedly as it brought back memories of the time I was fishing for mackerel, when we were regularly at anchor at St Michael's Mount, on the freezer Cordella, usually with a deckload of mackerel and processing in the factory.

So the season went on. March was approaching and so was the end of our time in Cornwall. As far as mackerel fishing was concerned, another successful and heavy fishing program had been achieved.

Rita and I had both enjoyed our stay in the hotel and felt a little unhappy as we prepared for our final days there.

Once again the catchers finished and were fully discharged to the Russians who prepared for departure from Falmouth to Murmansk or wherever they were going.

It was all over. After packing our gear and saying farewell to various friends, Rita and I left the Falmouth Hotel bound for Hessle. Another adventure had come to a close...

I spent the summertime at home waiting for orders concerning the next season. This time I was going to Ullapool earlier, around August. There was going to be a change in the accommodation when we started the operation that I would find out more about on my arrival.

I was ordered to report to Ullapool, this time to a house called Woollamalloo, just as you entered Ullapool. I made my way North along the usual route through Edinburgh, Perth and Inverness, then to Ullapool.

Woollamalloo was a large detached house overlooking Loch Broom, where David, Alistair and Derek of P and J and I would stay. It contained a large dining room, five bedrooms; two upstairs and three downstairs, a bathroom and a toilet downstairs, one toilet upstairs, one small room off the dining room and a kitchen.

The lady who owned the house, Margaret McGregor was a unique, old dear, who believe it or not had rented the house to our firm and was living in her caravan in the grounds.

I met this fine lady and she told me her life story, how she met her husband and how she worked later in life, helping her husband to operate his fishing boat, and turning out at four in the morning to assist landing the catch that he brought in.

She told me she met her husband while sailing in a steamship on the Australian run. Her husband was employed at the time as bosun on a ship named Woollamalloo.

For the remainder of the season she lived in the caravan and would not come inside for anything, drawing all her water from a tap outside and boiling it on her small stove. She went right through the winter like this. I used to spend many hours in her caravan just listening to her yarns about the hard, toiling life she'd had in her younger days.

I phoned Rita and gave her a full update on what was happening and about my meeting with Margaret McGregor. So now it was get aboard Woollamalloo and stand by for the mackerel season.

We were up early for the season and Ullapool in August seemed full of tourists. And as our normal Myrtle Cottage wasn't available until the end of September, I was going to start our operation from Woollamalloo. I commenced watch at about five in the morning in the base and was relieved by the rest of the staff coming back in the late afternoon.

We were operating with herring as well as mackerel, with the biggest part of the herring going to the pier market. We waited for the first boats to arrive with mackerel, some of the Eastern Block countries' factory vessels had arrived but not all of them. They would arrive as the season got underway properly.

We were still enjoying hot sunshine and exceptional weather in Ullapool. The heatwave had enveloped the highlands and the place had taken on a real holiday look. And as the season got underway, the first mackerel vessels arrived and I commenced my usual nightwatches that would go on until my first leave.

After about a month of operations the mackerel catches were increasing daily and soon we had the usual full boats arriving and the factory ships working at full capacity. Once again Ullapool was a hive of activity.

While the heatwave continued, I thought that I would bring Rita and my granddaughter Lisa, who was now twelve years old, up to Ullapool for a holiday. But accommodation was a problem. Everywhere was full with tourists but my good friend Danny Ross who owned the caravan site came to my rescue. When I told him of my intentions, he offered me one of his large caravans. This I thought would be just the thing, so I informed my wife that I would bring her and Lisa back with me after my next leave. But meanwhile it was on with the operation.

It now seemed to be full steam ahead for everyone, including my good friends John McLeod, the small grocer who was now fully engaged in supplying the Russians with stores, Harry McRae who was running a 24-hour boat service, back and forth to Annat Bay with supplies and personnel. And Charlie McDonald, the small supermarket owner who was now involved in supplying the Eastern Block ships. Ullapool was swinging.

Soon my leave, a long weekend from Thursday to Monday arrived. I drove back to Hull down my usual route, Inverness to Perth, then to Edinburgh, York and finally to Hessle.

I enjoyed a couple of days at home in the unbelievable weather. But when the heatwave showed no signs of coming to an end, on the Sunday I decided to take Rita and Lisa back to Ullapool as it was usually a quiet day for traffic and would undoubtedly be the best for travelling. We packed enough for a fortnight and set off. But boy, was it hot travelling?

When we arrived in Ullapool around teatime, I drove straight to the campsite. My close friend Danny met us there with the keys and showed us to the caravan. It was quite large but compact, with a bedroom, a toilet and dining space with a cooker and a refrigerator.

It overlooked the loch, where all movements of the fishing vessels could be seen. This was going to be our accommodation for the next two weeks. I was going to do nightwatch and therefore would have most of the day off.

We spent the first night in our new quarters and the following day I took them around Ullapool and showed them where the shops and the places of interest were. Then in the hardware store, I purchased a fishing rod and some tackle, then showed Lisa where she could sit on the pier and catch mackerel and other types of fish. From the base, I could watch how she was doing and how much she was catching...

The mackerel season carried on relentlessly day and night, seven days a week. And so did Lisa's holiday. She spent quite a bit of time on the pier fishing with her rod and tackle. And received an unexpected but lovely treat when Harry's boatmen took her out to the Russians in Annat Bay. First they took her alongside the Polish vessel Admiral Arkiseski, then to the big Russian factory ship Victor Kingisepp, before ending with a trip round the Summer Isles and then back in. From then onwards I took them to Loch Inver, Dingwall, Inverness and various other places of interest in the Highlands.

It was a great holiday for them, but when it had finished the problem was how to get them back home to Hessle. Fortunately one of our staff came to the rescue. Duncan, one of the new additions to our staff was going to be their escort. He was due his leave and as he lived in Hull he offered to take them both back.

All too soon the day arrived when they were to return to Hessle. I packed their gear and they prepared for their departure and trip home. It was then time to say goodbye to Rita and Lisa. Duncan duly arrived to pick them up and off they went.

Later in the day, when they had arrived in Hessle, after a journey of about 470 miles, Rita telephoned me to say she had got back. I thought that was quick. She then added that her hair had stood on end for much of the journey with Duncan's safe but 'Silverstone racing car speeds'.

So ended the holiday season, I would see them again on my next leave, about ten day's later. But meanwhile it was back to Klondiking.

As well as the Russians, Poles, Bulgarians and East Germans we now had some Dutch ships taking part in the operation with names such as Van Der Zwan, De Hocker and Schout Velthus. These ships were usually anchored in loch Broom just off Ullapool pier, all taking mackerel from the Scots' catchers. It was a huge project, all controlled from the base, 24 hours a day. And Myrtle Cottage was ready for occupation again as the tourist season had ended.

Meanwhile Harry McRae's boat service went from strength to strength. It was in constant demand, especially for the transporting of cartons and plastic bags to the Russian vessels. The cartons were later filled with the endless supply of mackerel being landed and eventually transported by refrigeration ship to destinations around the Northern Hemisphere. With this heavy workload, Harry had to invest in a bigger boat capable of handling this increased demand. So from bringing me ashore from Cordella as a single boatman himself, he was now in charge of a thriving and very successful boating business on the pier.

When Ray left us, we were joined by another J. Marr's radio operator from Hull, Alan Fulchard. Alan and I already knew each other well and for the next few years we worked together mainly on night shifts.

My friend, our Spanish part of the operation, Enrique, had been joined by Felix and Jose, who were of course all fluent in Russian. These gentlemen were of great help to us during the night watch, especially with any out of the ordinary problems, where we required their assistance with the Russian language. Normally I had no problem with the Russians as they seemed to understand my Scottish tongue compared with the English one. My name with them was 'Mr Bob'. After a while I got to know quite a few Russian words, such as 'Dobra vechea, Mr Bob,' which meant 'good day'.

It will now be apparent what Klondiking was all about. I have explained the operation in a condensed form but believe me this was a huge offshore market, working seasonally from September to March and only finishing when our quota of mackerel had been caught. This was indicated by orders from MAFF - Ministry of Agriculture and Fisheries - that we had caught our full quota allowed for that operation. Then it was time to pack up and wait until the next season.

And although I have explained the Klondiking operation from a radio officer's viewpoint, I must also emphasise that the managers of this huge enterprise had an even greater responsibility on their shoulders.

Decisions had to be made on the spot regarding this huge offshore market. In my early days I had observed this in Ullapool with two of the operational managers Nick and David who later on, rose to higher positions in the company. I learnt a lot from Nick and David on how Klondiking operated, from how to deal with delivery notes brought in from the fleet to dealing with fishery office procedure and many other aspects of the project.

Later on in my ten years of Klondiking I was going to be in Ullapool on my own, dealing with fish catchers, factory vessels and everything else appertaining to the operation.

The three operational managers who I would deal with in Ullapool were three captains from the big freezer trawlers who had joined us. David of course was one of the captains who I knew very well. We had sailed together on Northella to Newfoundland, Labrador, Greenland and the Barents Sea, and later in the Cordella to take fish from the Poles in the Baltic. I'd also sailed with Harry, another of the captains, on the Cordella for J. Marr. Whilst Tony, the third one, had joined us from another company, British United Trawlers.

So David was in charge, with Tony, Harry and myself and later Alan, a radio operator from the freezer Junella, all 'sea dogs'.

I moved back into Myrtle Cottage with Jerry, an ex-head cashier with Newington Trawlers.

So it was now back to work Klondiking. The season was in full swing with plenty of mackerel entering, so there were no quiet nights unless some stormy weather appeared...

Robert Baillie

CHAPTER 18
A NEW ERA

There was a significant change to my seasonal work in Ullapool. As Rita was on her own back home it was suggested to me that she could come up to Ullapool and stay in Myrtle Cottage for the seasonal work. Rita was delighted with this news as it would eliminate the long journey going home on leave each month. So on my next leave I would go home, pack up and both leave our home in Hessle and come to Ullapool.

Jerry moved out of Myrtle Cottage and across into Woolamalloo and Rita, with what seemed an immense amount of gear, moved in. Myrtle Cottage was going to be our abode every season for the next six years, September to March. We made our new home as comfortable as possible as we would be living there for at least five or six months of the year. We left our house in Hessle in the capable hands of our neighbour Irene.

Myrtle Cottage was owned by George and Rosanna Ross, relatives of the Mr Ross who had given us the caravan for Lisa and Rita's holiday. Over the next few years George and Rosanna were going to become our great friends, in fact we soon became what you would term 'locals' in Ullapool and met many new friends in the community.

Back at the pier and the base, we had some new names in the Dutch fleet operating with us including Alida, Ariadne, Prince Bernard, Cornelius Vrolik and Zeeland. And when the time came for me to retire I would have operated with many different nationalities including the Romanians and two Nigerian boats that had joined operation. Meanwhile, Jerry had left us and Alan Fulcher would replace him in the near future.

Rita and I were now resident in Ullapool for the

season. What a strange turn to my career this was compared to my 'fishing the Arctic' days...

We had now moved from our portacabin behind Charlie MacDonald's supermarket to the Seaforth Hotel overlooking the pier. Here we had taken over two of the top floor rooms to set up base in one, the other being used for general purposes. This was far more comfortable than our 'portacabin days' and included a toilet and a bathroom.

So it was on with the Klondiking operation with our staff, including Dave, Tony, Harry, Duncan, Jill, Ron and Betty in Ardmair House. Ron, our administrator and cashier who handled the delivery notes from the Eastern Block vessels and fishing boats after they had discharged their catches. Alisdair, Derek, Mike and old Davy. And Alan and I, the night duty operators.

The staff, fishing boat skippers and the shore side of the operation were all addressed by their first names. The reason for this was that with such a huge team operation there was no time for 'Yes sir, No sir,' here.

A lot of changes had occurred in the Ullapool Klondiking operation. For instance, a number of firms that had used our company to discharge their boats had now branched out on their own and had their own Russian vessels. And we had a new shipping agency company, 'Nordstar'.

Jill and Terry were responsible for all entries, departures of the factory vessels, reefers and various other shipping movements. And with well-known names such as 'Joint Trawlers/Scofish', 'Caley Fisheries', 'North Minch' and 'Falfish' all participating in the operation, it was quite a lively competition here for the season.

As well as pursers and trawlers taking part, we had the old brigade of pair trawlers. As the name suggests, these trawlers such as Quiet Waters, Steadfast Hope, Scottish Maid, Helena, Kimara and Uberous, operated in pairs with a huge net, towed astern, secured to each one by warps.

We now also had the southern Irish boats taking part in the mackerel fishing, with such names as Sheanne, Anya, Father McKee, Brendellen and Olgarry. We were going to have some fun with this competition, Scots versus Irish!

We also had the Rumanians operating with such names as Ciucas and Putna. They were mostly anchored off the pier taking mackerel, so there was quite an array of boats in Loch Broom and Annat Bay.

So it was on with the operation with fishing vessels calling from sea with ETAs, fishing vessels entering the bay and booking into base, then when cleared being directed to proceed to a Russian, Bulgarian, Polish, East German or Rumanian vessel, whoever was waiting for fish. And ships arriving and coming to the pier to wait their turn for landing, whenever a factory vessel was ready for fish.

Rita was now established in Myrtle Cottage and got a job looking after the boys' houses and cottages. She was now officially a company employee in charge of looking after their accommodation.

Our circle of friends increased continuously as Rita and I became regarded as 'locals' and Ullapool became a real home from home to us.

It included Alice, our next-door neighbour who was a great friend whenever we were 'in need'. Marilyn, who owned the guesthouse 'Loch View' near to Myrtle Cottage. Gordon, who owned the mobile fish and chip shop, Ian, the owner of the Argyle Hotel and my good friend John, the electrician who owned the shop where I rented my first washing machine. Billy McRae, a topline 'shellfisher' with his own boat. Ken, our next-door neighbour and manager of the 'Scottish Woollen' shop. Jackie McLeod and his wife Florence who in the early days looked after Myrtle Cottage. And Viv and Audrey, two stalwart lasses working in John McLeod's, who I used to keep updated on arrivals so that they could get plenty of orders for stores. The list could go on forever....

I look back at this period as undoubtedly one of the happiest times of my life. It was the first time that Rita and I had been together for such a lengthy period. Most of our early married life was spent apart as I sailed the Arctic and she sat at home waiting for me to return.

So to finish my watch at the base and be back at home in the cottage with Rita within a few minutes was great. I was learning to appreciate the benefits of this shoreman's life whilst still being heavily involved with 'a life at sea'.

To appreciate the magnitude of this huge operation we must compare it to the early days of the project when our company was the main handler of the fishing vessels and the Russian factory ships. Now, the Russian vessels still made up most of the fleet but were supplied by our fishing boats annexed to our company, as well as countless purse seiners, trawlers and pair trawlers, that were all fishing for mackerel to supply to the Eastern Block ships.

While in Ullapool Rita and I made a great friend with the fleet captain of the Bulgarians, Captain Kapzamalov, who was a great gentleman. His fleet consisted of the Albeno, Alushia, Bekas Argonaut, Kondor, Fizalia, Glarus, Flamingo and Kaprelia.

Captain Kapzamalov became a regular visitor to our cottage where Rita would always have a coffee ready and we would then listen to his many interesting yarns especially about his family. The captain was of great value to our company particularly in very heavy fishing where we were looking for all available space to land mackerel. There were some nights when we had a glut of mackerel arrive but there was no free space at the Russian vessels. When this happened I would call Captain Kapzamalov and he would give me maybe three or four of his vessels. I could then move some of my fishing vessels waiting to land and probably get rid of 100 to 200 ton.

So life went on in Ullapool, with Rita enjoying her new job with the company, looking after the boys' accommodation and making sure it was all up to scratch. It was quite a laugh with some of the lads when she was due at their house or cottage as they furiously tried to clear things away and tidy up ready for her arrival.

Some of the places that she attended were the detached house, 'Woollamallo', the cottage 'Arkle', the large house 'Admair' and the company's headquarters on Shore Street. As well as looking after these and many other properties, she had other duties to do, such as she would have regular visits from some of the lads who wanted their shirts ironed or maybe some washing done.

I remember one amusing incident when our Spanish Rep. came to ask Rita if she could wash and iron some 'T' shirts for him. It was really funny to watch as Felix stood in front of her, gesticulating and trying to explain in his broken English what he required.

After two or three weeks, Rita ended up with a cottage full of boxes of chocolates and bottles of wine from a grateful crowd of lads highly satisfied with this invaluable new service…

I had a communication set in Myrtle Cottage so that I could always be in contact with the Russian vessels. And as Rita listened to the messages all day, she soon found that she was picking up quite a few words of Russian during her stay there.

She had now settled into this new life in the Highlands that took her away from 'home' for five months of the year including Christmas and New Year.

For the next six years this was our home during September and March. During these long winter months, apart from the mail and the weekly telephone call to our dear friend and neighbour Irene, we seemed to lose touch with a lot of what was happening back in Hessle.

When not on duty we spent a lot of time walking around the lochs and driving into Dingwall and Inverness to do some shopping. And when the rest had gone home for the holidays, we remained in our cottage and enjoyed the peace and quiet of the highland Christmas and the happiest of New Years.

A great change was taking place regarding mackerel fishing. The great abundance of mackerel that had been predominant in the past was declining fast. Boats which were previously only away for a few hours before returning with their catches were now having to travel further afield, right down to the south of the Isle of Skye.

At one time mackerel had been thick and heavy from Cape Wrath down to Skye but now there seemed very little between those two positions. More alarming was the fact that mackerel that normally moved south from the Shetlands to the Minch were remaining around the Shetlands and not moving south at all. This meant that all boats fishing for mackerel around Shetland had a long steam back to Ullapool for discharge. This didn't affect the purse seiners so much with their frozen tanks but trawlers normally after steaming this longer distance were more prone to their fish going off, especially if they also had a long wait for discharge.

So it looked likely that part of the Russian fleet would move to anchor in the Shetlands close to where the mackerel shoals were. This affected Ullapool in one way. When the mackerel was in the Minch, boats were arriving for discharge regularly, resulting in stacking up with waiting lists. But now with the mackerel being much further away, waiting lists would be a thing of the past. We still had quite a bit of mackerel arriving though, mostly from the larger pursers carrying quite big tonnages.

The great advantage that Ullapool had compared to Lerwick was the fact Ullapool's Annat Bay was an ideal closed-in bay whereas Lerwick was open to the fierce weather conditions. So if the weather worsened and the winds increased from the north, the factory vessels might have to up anchor and move south to take fish on board. Also there was not the anchorage space available at Lerwick that Annat Bay had.

So that was how it was heading. Part of the fleet was at Lerwick and the major part of it at Ullapool. This also resulted in the staff splitting with some working in Lerwick and others in Ullapool. But it was definitely Ullapool for Rita and me. Carry on Klondiking...

As the season progressed, we had another change when the Ullapool part of the operation closed early but the Lerwick part carried on after yet another move, this time to Southern Ireland. The factory ships, fishing vessels and staff went to Killybegs in Southern Ireland where from March to May, the operation continued but on a reduced scale to the Ullapool one.

It was during this transfer that Rita and I found ourselves left in Ullapool on our own, to clear up the remaining fishing vessels that were still landing in Ullapool and seeing to the departures of the factory vessels back to Russia. It was only after all the ships had been cleared that we prepared for our return to Hessle.

We packed up the car, checked our cottage and the base, then handed the base keys to Donnie the harbourmaster and the cottage keys to Rosanna. We bid goodbye to all our friends and with a 'See you next season,' we were off.

We did not do the full journey but stopped in a little hotel in Lauderdale, south of Edinburgh for the night. After an evening meal, a good night's sleep and a leisurely breakfast, we were on our way again heading south. We always stopped at the cemetery in the grounds of Jedburgh Castle to put some flowers on my mother's grave. Then it was over the Cheviot Hills and for the first time in five months, England!

'Not a bad adventure?' said Rita, already looking forward to the next season.

So onto the A1, then York and finally to Hessle. Some new neighbours had moved in while we had been away, they probably thought we were just moving in. Rita and I went round to thank Irene and her husband Mike who had looked after our house religiously and then to see the family with a little dram of my best whiskey.

We were now at home again until September when we would return to Ullapool for another season. And I couldn't help but think that our stay was only temporary...

During my time at sea, I'd always thought that when I retired I would like an allotment to try my hand at gardening, growing our own vegetables and of course enjoying the open-air. I had applied to Hessle Town Council for one and was surprised when the Town Clerk called and said, 'I'm pleased to tell you that you've been allocated a 300 square yard allotment.'

Robert Baillie

My God, I thought, this is not going to be 'an easy bit of gardening'.

But anyway, I went across to view my new allotment. It didn't have a shed so the first thing we did was to get one. We also bought some tools, plant-pots and some garden furniture and were now ready to start work. We then purchased some vegetable plants, including potatoes, carrots etc., and in they went. Then we sat back and waited for nature to take its course.

So my summer at home was taken up with this new venture, with Rita coming across with the sandwiches and tea each day. It was great stuff.

The summer went by very quickly and all too soon it was time to start thinking about returning to Scotland. And sure enough, on September 1 our operations director called with orders for Rita and I to move back to Ullapool. So quick packing and arranging for house to be looked after we had packed and was now driving north once again the usual route; York, A1 Edinburgh, Perth and Inverness,then to Ullapool and back to our second home Myrtle Cottage, which was now a prepared base for operations. Stand by for the Russian, Bulgarian, East German, Polish and Romanian fishing fleets that were already making for the fishing grounds. Here, it was back into full swing mackerel fishing and Rita too with her housekeeping operations.

Everything was going well until December when we suffered a calamity. On Tuesday, December 10, I drove to Dingwall to pick up a health certificate for one of the Russian vessels. While there Rita and I did some Christmas shopping and around noon set off back for Ullapool. The weather was dry but the temperature had dropped to zero. As I continued on my journey, the weather deteriorated and there was a slight fall of sleet and the roads started to freeze. As I drove out of Strassepeffer near Jamestown we hit some black ice, went off the road and down the embankment. Then, as we came back onto the main road I was hit by a car sliding on ice from the opposite direction.

Rita and I got out and luckily had no serious injuries but my new Escort was a write-off.

The Strassepeffer police picked us up and two) to Strathpeffer we then booked in the Richmond hotel till we recovered the police brought our gear and I phoned the AA who recovered my car and took it to a Dingwall garage. Meanwhile we were informed that more than twenty cars had gone off the road with a few write-offs being reported. So we stopped the night in the Richmond Hotel and at 11am the next morning Duncan arrived to take us back to Ullapool.

The weather had improved greatly with no icy roads to deal with, but after the disaster we left Ullapool on Saturday December 14 on the 07.50 Inverness to York train.

At 15.45 we arrived at Hull and were picked up by Irene, our 'house protector' who drove us to Hessle.

It was now Christmas week but with no car. So I set about getting another. Hunting around, I found one, a Mazda 323, 1.3 hatchback. It was the same year as my 'write-off' but with less mileage. So with a cheque from my insurance company for my Escort, a quick deal was done and I had a Mazda.

I spent the Christmas and New Year break at home and after the celebrations it was back to Ullapool for the remainder of the season, which ended in March. Then it was back again to Hessle where I once more set about working on my allotment.

In early July Rita and I went to stay in a cottage in Jedburgh for the town's festival for eight days.

The remainder of our leave was spent mostly on our allotment. We now had a fine, new shed, a table and some chairs, and a canopy to shield us from the sun.

Robert Baillie

And with a picnic basket packed with salad, sandwiches, cakes and cool drinks, Rita and I enjoyed most days over there...

On September 17 I was instructed to prepare for another season in Ullapool but this time I would be on my own for the first month.

I was asked to take a company car from Hull to Ullapool and on the way to pick up my close friend David Hinchcliffe from his home. We were both then to proceed to Scotland ready for the start of the season. So on Friday, September 19 I picked up David and proceeded north. David of course was the manager of operations at Ullapool and for a short time we would both be living in Myrtle Cottage.

We arrived at Ullapool at 18:30 hours and after dropping our gear in Myrtle Cottage got ready to have a look at the base at the Seaforth Hotel and prepare to re-start the operation.

The Russians, Bulgarians, East Germans, Poles and Romanians were either already anchored or were arriving on September 21.

My first watch in base was midnight until 04.00 hours then 08.00 to 2100 hours. The usual procedure was soon underway again with catchers coming in with mackerel, discharging to the Russian and other Eastern Block ships all controlled from base. Then every day after that, it was a watch from 08.00 to 19:00 hours up till September 30 where it changed to 21.00 to 07:30 hours in the morning.

One unfortunate incident that took place during this period was the loss of the company car that I had carefully nursed since I had returned to Ullapool from Hessle before the start of the season.

On an official business trip to Dingwall, the lad driving the car encountered a deer that bounded out into the road and tried to jump over the bonnet of the car. This unfortunately resulted in the driver swerving, going off the road and down the embankment and the car was a complete write-off.

On Monday, October 20 my leave was due. Davey from 'P and J' drove me to Inverness Station and I was back in Hessle by 4pm. I informed Rita to prepare to leave for Ullapool on Saturday, October 25 and the next few days were spent getting the car serviced, packing and handing over the house to Irene. Then at 09.00 on Saturday I once again left for Ullapool and at 16:00 hours booked into the Bull Hotel in Lauderdale for the night. It was approximately halfway between Hessle and Ullapool so after an evening meal, a good night's sleep and a hearty breakfast we left the Bull at 9.30am and continued on our journey north.

By 15:00 hours we were back in Myrtle cottage. I left Rita to unpack and get everything in order while I went along to the Argyle Hotel to let everyone know that I was back. I had a pint and a yarn with the locals then reported to base. And at midnight I was back on night watch, which I would do continuously, including Saturdays and Sundays.

The following day, Rita was also back at work, carrying out her housekeeping duties in the staff's accommodation. She now had a crucial part in the operation...

Everything did not run smoothly all the time. I don't refer to our operation but to the effects of the weather. First of course it affected the fish catchers, which could not fish in foul weather. In our experience in Ullapool, the winds could reach 90 mph and with the addition of snowstorms this had a far-reaching effect. We could suddenly find that our electricity supply had been cut off, which resulted in all our communications' equipment being rendered out of action, with no contact with the ships at sea or the Eastern Block ships in the bay.

Another thing that could be affected was Myrtle Cottage, which was all-electric, including the fires, cooker and washers etc. But here was where our highland neighbours came to our help. Whenever the electricity was cut off, our very good friend and next door neighbour, Alice McGregor, would arrive at the door with some candles, a paraffin heater and a kettle full of boiling water from her gas stove. So although we had to 'rough it', at least we could heat up a can of beans to have with a bit of bread and butter and the hot kettle made a mug of tea. What more could you ask for?

When the storm had abated and the electric was reconnected, it was back to Klondiking, pickup where we had left off and start to get the ships organised again. This went on until December when once again the staff and the catchers went home, and Rita and I were left in charge.

After the last catches had been discharged and the delivery notes dealt with, we more or less closed down until the Irish arrived back with mackerel on New Year's Eve. The southern Irish only celebrated Christmas and were out fishing again by the New Year. But now it was time to prepare for Christmas.

Some of the large Russian ships that were remaining wanted Christmas trees sent out. We saw to this plus all the other fare. Rita and I had purchased a proper highland fir for a Christmas tree and with a few decorations our cottage was transformed.

Over the period quite a few of the locals who we had made friends with over the years came to see us. Rita had baked her own Christmas cake, so with a hamper from John McLeod's containing the turkey, we were ready.

WAITING FOR THE TIDE

December 23 was our wedding anniversary. I booked a table at the Morefield Motel and always remember sitting in the restaurant enjoying the evening out, without a care in the world and with no watch-keeping to think about. Great stuff!

We then enjoyed the whole of Christmas Day in our cottage overlooking Loch Broom. We had our dinner with all the trimmings and a bottle of wine, plus a Christmas pudding.

It was certainly a change to some of the Christmas dinners I had during my Arctic days, with the ship rolling from side to side in zero temperatures. But now it was quiet and laid-back, with a visit from our two great friends Jackie and Florence McLeod, and a few drams.

This was Christmas. On Boxing Day, we again had a few friends round and Rita made a lovely tea. Then afterwards we went to the Argyle Hotel and a good night was had by all.

It was then time to sit back and wait for our Irish catchers to arrive on December 29…

Robert Baillie

CHAPTER 19
ULLAPOOL

In January 1988, our base in Ullapool was moved from the Seaforth Hotel to a house in Shore Street, owned by Rosanna Ross. It was quite a large, three-bedroom house and one of the rooms downstairs had been converted into our new base. Although it had all the normal communications' equipment my nightwatches were carried out from a small office on Ullapool pier. But at the start of the year, the very stormy weather with force nine, southwest winds, was affecting the whole operation and most of my watches were done from Myrtle Cottage.

Tuesday, January 5 was the start of the fishing season but to make matters worse we had a full power cut from 18.00 to 03.00 the next morning. The stormy weather continued right through the week and lasted for the rest of the month. By Sunday, January 24 all ships were at anchor due to the northeast gales and there was no fish arriving in Ullapool.

On February 1 the weather had hit us very badly with only small amounts of herring arriving. The information now was that most ships had left and were now at Rathmullen in Ireland. By Saturday, February 6 all the Rumanians had left and the big Russian vessel Rybatskayaslava was also leaving, bound for Falmouth.

Tony our manager was away and eventually would also go to Ireland. David was in America and Canada in charge of operations over there. Funnily enough he was in Yarmouth, Nova Scotia where I had done all my flight training during the war as a Telegraphist-Air Gunner in the Fleet Air Arm.

Eventually I was informed that I would be left on

my own with two Russians, The Ledus and Tikorest. I would have the pair trawlers, Golden Sceptre and Quiet Waters with Captain Albert, who would be fetching only herring to supply these two Russians. As the pair trawlers usually arrived at around 03.00 each morning I had a continuous watch at Myrtle Cottage, only going to the pier office to send and receive faxes or to deal with any problems with the two Russian captains.

So right up to February 26, I had Quiet Waters and Golden Sceptre coming in with herring. Old Albert was a very experienced skipper and knew every ground in the Minch. He was a top herring fishermen and every morning around 03.00 hours I would get a telephone call with his unmistakable voice saying, 'Marr's base, this is Quiet Waters,' and his ETA. Quiet waters would go to Tikaresk and Golden Sceptre to Ledus. It was very successful and quite a bit of herring was landed.

I had one call from my old friend Joe Lovin, who was in charge of the Shetland fishing boats asking had I space for one mackerel boat and this was arranged.

By Friday, February 26 all the Russians except Ledus and Tikaresk had left, some to Ireland and it was then announced that the fishing season in Ullapool had closed. Then on Saturday 27, storm force, northerly winds and snow blizzards.

I had to wind up operations with my two Russians, get all their papers, customs, fishery office clearances with the Nordstar shipping agent and also all their delivery notes of the amount of herring put on board. Only when all this had been completed, were they allowed to leave Ullapool. Then the only boats that remained for me to clear were Quiet Waters and Golden Sceptre. They would then leave for home after doing a great job for me throughout the herring season. Finally, I prepared to clear the pier base and Belle Vue, our base in Shore Street.

Robert Baillie

The last captain to come into base was our old friend Captain Kapzamalov as the Bulgarians returned the communication equipment that we had lent them.

The only things left to do was make an itinerary of all the equipment we had in Ullapool and phone Ron, the telephone engineer to come and remove the phones. Rita meanwhile was attending to her cottages and the Belle Vue base. So that was it, the end of another season. Myrtle Cottage was all quiet now and I was on holiday until my next call.

On Saturday, March 5 after bidding goodbye to all our friends until the next season, we left Ullapool at 09.30 bound for Hessle. But we were not going straight home, we were stopping off in Jedburgh, my home town. We took the usual route through Inverness, Perth and Edinburgh and eventually at 16:00 hours arrived in Jedburgh and booked into the Kenmore Bank Guesthouse for the night. And at 11am the next day we left for Hessle and arrived back home at 17:00 hours.

I planned to spend most of the summer on my allotment where I had ordered a new shed to be erected. This kind of life was all new to me. But I transferred the garden tools and furniture into the shed and was soon ready for planting the vegetables.

So Rita and I spent most of the summer across on the allotment enjoying the sunny weather and watching the growth of our impressive crop of vegetables. But on Tuesday, August 23, I was summoned to Marr International's office and informed that two days later I was going to Lerwick in the Shetland's, Klondiking herring.

So the following day I went down to the dock to collect the train and ferry tickets and at 07.20 on the Thursday morning I left Hessle station for York and arrived at Aberdeen at 2pm. Here I was informed that I had to take a Ford Escort company car onto the ferry to

WAITING FOR THE TIDE

Lerwick.

Before that however, I went to visit my father and sister and her husband Jim in Aberdeen. Jim then drove me to the ferry, where at 17:00 hours I boarded the ferry. I saw that the car was stowed safely and then made my way to my cabin and waited for sailing time.

When we arrived at Lerwick at 08.00 the following morning, I was shown to my accommodation, a nice flat overlooking the harbour. And better still, just down a flight of stairs was a big takeaway, so that was my food taken care of.

Our base was a portacabin on Alexander Wharf where our catchers came alongside with their catches and a sample was taken out to the Russians anchored off Lerwick. But this position was not as protected from the weather as Ullapool. You had anchorage at 'North and South roads' so if a northerly gale was in force, the Russians anchored in the 'North Road' would have to lift anchor and move south in order to provide a lee for discharging the catchers.

The herring fishing operation in Lerwick concentrated almost entirely on herring roe. Scottish herring roe was a delicacy for the Japanese so there were numerous Japanese buyers in Lerwick, each one allocated to a Russian vessel.

The procedure was when a catcher arrived at the wharf, I would telephone the hotel where the Japanese buyers were staying. They would come to the wharf and take a sample of the herring roe and if it was acceptable, we would direct this catcher to the buyer's Russian vessel. Of course there was more than one Japanese company's buyers in Lerwick, so we had to make sure that we did not send the catcher to the wrong ship.

The Russians allocated to the Japanese would process this herring, pack it into cartons and get it ready for transporting in a refrigeration ship to Japan.

Robert Baillie

This went on 24 hours a day, seven days a week.

We had some of our old Klondiking names here including the Russians, Rybatskayaslava, Kapagory and Vyshgorod, plus the Scots' pursers Christina S., Coronella, Sedulous and Omega.

I was now working constantly on nightshifts, 22.00 to 08.00.

As most of the herring came in during the night I found myself calling the Japanese Reps around 03.00 in the morning. They were always there, right on time, down to the quayside to test the sample of roe. If everything was okay, I would call the Russian factory ship and inform him of the name of the catcher that was coming to him and what quantity of herring he had.

When I finished my watch at 08.00 it was straight to a dockside cafe for a couple of bacon rolls and take them back to the flat to enjoy with a pot of tea, then retire.

At teatime I went down to the takeaway where I could choose from fish and chips, pie and chips or black pudding and white pudding and chips or chicken and chips, all served with bread rolls. This was great, ready made meals literally on my doorstep.

Thursday, September 8 was my birthday. I was 64 years old and had been working for 50 years.

The herring season had finished in Lerwick so it was just a matter of clearing up the existing boats.

I left Lerwick on the following Monday. This time I had to take a company car back to Aberdeen and drop it at P & J Johnstone's fish dock. But at 16.00 hours as I boarded the ferry Sunnyva there was almost a terrible calamity, when I was directed not onto the main deck but up a narrow ramp onto a small one.

I attempted to drive up the ramp but because the car was loaded with a lot of heavy gear in the boot this was impossible and it nearly slid over the side. Realising the problem, one of the crewmen got me to reverse back and moved me onto the main deck.

Once I was safely parked, I made my way to my reserved cabin but when I entered it, there was another problem. Somebody was already in it!

I quickly introduced myself to the gentleman in 'my' cabin and found that he was Charlie Durno, a farmer from Netherdale Turriff in Aberdeenshire. There had seemingly been a 'double-booking' but when I realised that he would have to leave despite there being plenty of room for two, I said to him, 'It's okay with me if you don't mind sharing.'

He replied that he didn't mind at all, so after a quick wash I changed and we proceeded to the bar where we had quite a yarn.

The next morning at breakfast I said to Charlie that I had always fancied a holiday in the area. And I was most surprised when he replied that he had an empty cottage on his land that he was only too glad to give us for a holiday any time in the summer.

This I accepted, so after exchanging addresses we bid each other goodbye.

When we docked in Aberdeen I collected the company car and made my way ashore and round to the fish dock where a very nice secretary in the P and J office said she would drive me to the station.

At 09.50 I boarded the train for York and enjoyed a pleasant journey and a dram or two chatting to some oilmen from the North Sea oilrigs about our experiences in Scotland. And at 16.45 I arrived at Hessle station and as there were no taxis, I walked home.

Another episode had come to a close.

It was now time to return to my allotment until further orders. The weather was very warm so Rita and I spent quite a lot of time across at the allotment,

Robert Baillie

hoeing, digging and planting, and frequently 'dining out' in front of the shed. Rita had become quite an expert with the hoe and up until September 29 we were fully occupied growing our vegetables although we realised that time was running out and we expected our orders soon. And sure enough, on Friday, September 30, David phoned and instructed Rita and I to proceed to Ullapool for the start of a new season.

We left for Ullapool the next morning at 09.00 and by 17.00 we had booked in the Lauderdale Hotel for the night. The following day we left Lauderdale bound for Ullapool and arrived at Myrtle Cottage at 15.45, unpacked our gear and got settled in. And on the Monday we were down at the base to commence the season mackerel fishing.

At first things were fairly quiet with very little fish arriving. The Russian vessel Rybatskayaslava was already there along with Ledus and Latvia and the Bulgarians Milenita, Ophelia, Glarusa and Limoza. We also had a newcomer, the Russian 'Novator'. This was a fine, new vessel and to commence his voyage he was anchored what they termed 'through the narrows' from Loch Broom to the Inner Loch that was beautifully landlocked.

My orders were that the first vessel arriving with mackerel would go straight to Novator. This happened to be my great friend George in Star Crest and was he amazed when he saw this great new vessel that at first glance looked like a big, sleek yacht rather than a fishing vessel. But it proved to be a much sought-after boat to discharge into with all the Scots' pursers. A little later the Russians Vasilisen, Andrey Audrev and Promislovik and the Germans Edward Claudius, Bruno Apitz, Granite and Stubnitz joined the operation.

We soon had the Scottish, plus the Southern Irish fishermen arriving with a heavy catch of fish. Things were hotting up. It was now back in full swing and I was on full night watch.

On Thursday, October 27 a new law presented the catchers with a bit of a problem to sort out. A law had been introduced regarding fishing limits and stated that no fishing for mackerel could take place to the west of 4° longitude. The fishermen had gone home for a meeting to discuss the problem. And the current situation was that the boats fishing in the prohibited area were now having trouble with gunboats trying to enforce the new rule.

Eventually, on Thursday, November 3 the bigger pursers started to arrive with the first mackerel. But the fish had been caught around the Shetlands, east of 4° longitude, and a long way from Ullapool.

On Friday, November 25 I was asked to take three Russian captains, one of them was the captain and owner of the Novator, to Inverness, then on a tour of Loch Ness and the 'Monster' area.

So at 9am I set off and drove them first to Inverness for a shopping spree. I dropped them at the main shopping area and left them to browse around, indicating what time I would pick them up and move on to Loch Ness. After an hour of shopping, I drove them to the loch and told them the legend of the Loch Ness Monster.

The laugh was that when I had finished, the Captain of the Novator who spoke perfect English asked. 'Bob, is it true that there is a monster?'

I replied, 'Well, it all depends on how much whiskey you have drunk whether you will see it or not.'

On our way back to Ullapool, I stopped at an old, isolated hunting Inn, surrounded by rolling green hills. Inside there was a big open log fire and hunting scenes, a stag's head and antlers on the wall.

Robert Baillie

I ordered each of them a roast beef sandwich and a pint of good Scottish beer and they all appeared very impressed. And we then returned to our base in Ullapool, where my three Russian captains were eager to thank everyone for a splendid day out...

In the first week of December 1988 we had a lot of mackerel arriving and quite a fleet of Eastern Block ships waiting for it. These included the Bulgarians; Sagitta, Kondor, Afala, Ophelia, Alka and Glarus, and the Russians, Trudovyaslava, Vasilisen, Latvia and and Sviatagor. Also in the operation we now had some Dutch ships taking mackerel and our own freezer, Westella, klondiking as well as our faithful pursers and pair trawlers, Kings X, Cristina S, Coronella, Orcadius Viking, Star Crest, Quiet Waters and Steadfast Hope, and the Irish boats. It was quite a mix of nationalities and all were very welcome.

I must also give another mention to the work done by my great friend, Harry McRae. Harry had now set up a thriving service to the fleet anchored in Loch Broom and Annat Bay. He now had quite a number of staff working for him at his base on the pier. This work was very essential to the operation, transporting cartons, plastic bags, packing tape, brails and of course the crews, to and from the ships. In fact, his company undertook all the transport that was moving between the pier and the fleet. It was a vast change to when I was first introduced to him.

Although there was plenty of mackerel being landed, things had been 'tightened up' by MAFF, (Ministry of Agriculture and Fisheries).

Each catcher entering the port had to call direct into the main fishing office in Ullapool and wait for a fishery officer to go out to them to check their catch before they could proceed to discharge to the Russian factory ship. Their fish tanks were thoroughly dipped to make sure that the amount they had booked in was correct, and only then could they proceed.

The fishing and discharging went on until December 10 when some very stormy weather arrived and resulted in no fishing and no entries.

The boats were fishing in a position 60° N. 04° W. but the storm had stopped them altogether. The only boats arriving back at Ullapool with any fish were the lucky ones who had caught their voyage before the storm started. Those who had managed it included Christina S, Omega and Orcadius Viking. So by Thursday, December 15 most of the Russians were leaving for Christmas and the New Year and the following day the pursers also started heading home.

The storm was growing in Annat Bay and we just hoped that we could discharge the few vessels that were arriving. We managed to clear Quo Vadis, Christina S and Coronella but things were getting bad in the bay for discharging. Omega and Orcadius Viking were being discharged to the Bulgarians. You can imagine the scene, the catcher alongside the factory ship, the stormy weather and the rise and fall of the sea threatening the possibility of damage to the catcher. It was a great relief when we heard that they had managed to discharge and were going home. But I had another problem.

Two of the smaller boats, Scottish Maid and Steadfast Hope, could not discharge unless the factory ship lifted anchor and moved to a better lee. This was finally achieved and the two little boats, despite rising up and down like corks, managed to discharge their catches.

The storm was so great now that the big Soviet ship, the Trudovyaslava, had to lift anchor, leave the bay and go out into the Minch to dodge head to wind. He just could not hold his anchor while in the bay. He would have dragged and possibly ran aground. It was a very precarious position to be in.

By December 22, we had cleared everyone but another storm was approaching with very high winds blowing ashore.

During this storm, Rita was doing the rounds of her houses. At Bellevue House on Shore Street, which faced the sea, huge seas were pounding over the wall and winds of nearly 90 mph were battering it. So the best thing was to get out of it and go home.

By Friday, December 23 all the staff had gone home. Only Rita and I were left. It was our wedding anniversary, 38 years married and we could not get out...

The stormy weather continued over Christmas, with not much chance of getting outside the cottage but fortunately we had everything 'on board'. Our Christmas tree lights were shining brightly and the turkey was roasting in the oven when suddenly another power cut left us with no electricity. We immediately had a visit from Alice with the usual paraffin stove but she had only been there for a few minutes when the electricity came back on and our Christmas dinner was saved.

After the Christmas celebrations we were on standby again for the Irish boats arriving back around December 29. They all returned to Ullapool by New Year's Eve except for 'Sheanne'. But as we started to worry what had happened to him, we were informed by our shipping agent that he had engine trouble and would not be arriving after all.

Rita and I had been invited round by our neighbour, Marlene, who owned the guesthouse, 'Loch View'. We had a good night there and saw in the New Year in great style.

WAITING FOR THE TIDE

1989 promised to be a very special year for me as on September 8 I would reach the age of 65 and after working for 51 years, I was officially due to retire.

On January 2, 1989 two Irish boats, Paula and Challenge came in with their first catches and after the normal entry procedure were directed to discharge to Poznikov and Teudovayaslava in Annat Bay. The following day, my relief Captain Harry Harrison arrived. He took over and I had the day off but stormy weather arrived again and we were once again storm bound with no watches no boats arriving.

On Friday, January 6 the storm abated and I resumed my nightwatch, 22.00 to 08:00 hours. We then received information from the fishing grounds, position 60° N 02° W that there was plenty of mackerel coming in and by Sunday 8 we were full of mackerel in Ullapool.

The boats continued to arrive with full capacity of mackerel right up to Thursday, January 12 when once again a full southwest storm appeared and all fishing boats were anchored with no fishing.

This stormy weather continued up to Thursday, January 19 but the next day the storm had abated and the boats had gone to sea to position 59° 38 N. 05°.16 W. and fishing in a depth of 60 fathoms. We then had reports of good fishing on this position and the first boats arrived back in Ullapool on Saturday 21 with plenty of mackerel aboard.

The other news was that mackerel was now down the west side of the Hebrides. Our ship, the freezer Westella, who had been taking mackerel, was now bound home with a full ship. This continued until Friday 27, when once again severe gales stopped all fishing.

On Wednesday, February 1 one or two boats

attempted to go out but hampered by the stormy weather soon returned to the safety of the port.

By Monday, February 6 the winds had decreased, the boats had returned to the fishing grounds and by Saturday, February 11 we had once again plenty of mackerel arriving. But again it was short lived as we soon received a forecast of more strong winds increasing to storm force from the northwest.

By the Sunday the last of our mackerel boats had landed their catches and all the crews had gone home. There was no nightshift only a day watch due to the stormy conditions.

On Monday 13 at 06:00 hours we were being battered by a full, northwest storm and by midday a hurricane was blowing with wind speeds of 106 mph recorded. There was a lot of structural damage done and at 18:00 hours we had reports that three boats had dragged their anchors and ran ashore.

By Saturday 18 the storm was still raging. Some of the larger Russian ships anchored in Annat Bay had gone out into the Minch to dodge and some of the fishing boats making their way to Barra Head had anchored in Loch Swilly.

On Tuesday, February 21 a number of the German Klondikers had gone to Ireland as we received reports that the mackerel was now down the Irish coast.

We were still recording winds in excess of 100 mph and some of our boats were storm bound in Rathmullen.

On Saturday, March 4 the Russians were leaving for Ireland and Captain Tony Atkins was out in Annat Bay signing them off. They then went to Ireland and Tony and Harry accompanied them to take part in the next operation. And Rita and I were once again left on our own.

I had to clear Ullapool of the boats that remained

and of course Rita had to ensure that all her houses were left in order now that another season was coming to an end.

Wednesday, March 8 was the end of the mackerel fishing season in Ullapool and Captain Harry Harrison left for Ireland. We were going through the procedure of closing down Ullapool. Rita was seeing to the company's accommodation and I made an inventory of all the communication sets and gear that would be stored until the next season and all the delivery notes and general paperwork that would be taken back to Hull.

A week later, Rita and I also finally left Ullapool after wishing all our friends goodbye until the following season. But would I return?

I was due to retire in the September and would just have to wait and see what happened…

On the journey home we stopped in my hometown of Jedburgh as we always did to put flowers on my mother's grave, situated in the castle grounds.

When we arrived back in Hessle on Thursday, March 16, we had been away in Ullapool for nearly six months. It had been a long season.

The next day I reported for the usual 'debriefing' to Marr's new headquarters in Livingston Road. It was a beautiful building for a company with a new name, 'Andrew Marr International'.

This was possibly going to be end of my working life. During the summer I would have to decide what to do. I may have to start to plan my retirement. But for now it was time to get across to the allotment and attend to the gardening and planting.

By May the weather had become very warm and it got even hotter by June. We started to think about a summer holiday and I remembered the offer of the

Robert Baillie

cottage from my friend Charlie Durno, the farmer from the northeast of Scotland who I met on the Lerwick to Aberdeen ferry. I got in touch with Charlie and 'Yes', he said, the cottage was available. So I arranged for Rita and I to go there for a holiday starting on Saturday, June 17. Meanwhile, until our holiday, I spent most of the time at the allotment or with my daughter and granddaughter who had moved to a house in Hessle about a mile from us.

On Saturday, June 17 at 06:00 hours, we set off for Scotland with the car packed full of clothes and provisions. I decided to take Rita on 'the scenic route' so with the weather still very hot, around 80°, I made my way to Edinburgh, then Perth and over the Grampians, coming down past the Queen's residence, Balmoral Castle, then into Ballater, where it was so hot, nearly 90°. We stopped to buy a few essential items, then drove on to Netherdale. Here we searched for our cottage, called 'Damfolds'. We knew roughly where it was situated but I had actually driven passed it.

Then suddenly Rita shouted, 'There it is!'

And there it was! Standing by itself in the middle of the most beautiful countryside, with an old barn on one side and a stream running by on the other. A little paradise surrounded by cornfields.

We drove up the dusty driveway and got out of the car. Then as we approached the front door, we saw a bunch of keys and a note saying: 'To Bob and Rita from Hessle. Welcome, Charlie.' We had only been there a couple of minutes when Charlie arrived with a large bottle of cold orange juice and a dozen fresh farm eggs. Our holiday had begun.

We visited Balmoral Castle and I took a trip up to Banff where our Scots purser fishermen lived. We also toured all the northeast of Scotland and visited my father, my sister Ren, and her husband Jim in Aberdeen. The weather remained so hot that we usually had breakfast outside in front of our cottage overlooking the cornfields. The climax to our holiday was a visit to Charlie's farmhouse for a night out with dinner and drinks. It was fantastic way to end one of the greatest holidays I ever had.

On Saturday, July 1 at 10.30am, we left 'Damfolds' bound for home. I took a different route home via Banchory, Brechin, Forfar, Dundee, Perth and Edinburgh, then Lauderdale Hotel, Jedburgh and York and finally on Sunday July 2 at 19:00 hours, we arrived back in Hessle.

It had been a wonderful holiday. Now I had to find out if I was retiring on September 8 or was I still required to go back to Ullapool?

The weather was very hot, up to 90° and it was reported to be the hottest July since records began. We spent our time on our allotment but the drought had brought in the order 'No hosepipes allowed' so it was a tough job watering 300 square yards of land with only water cannons. But one great thing I remember was that we enjoyed a lot of picnics in front of our shed. There was certainly no need to go abroad for the sunshine, we'd got it here...

My granddaughter Lisa had now left school and was employed in a big supermarket, where she was in charge of the delicatessen and doing very well.

This was my official retirement year. It seemed a very long time since at the age of 18 in 1942 I had begun my sea career with the Fleet Air Arm during World War II. And following 43 years associated with the Hull Deep Sea fishing fleet including nine years with the Klondike fleet in Ullapool, I started to wonder what I would do after I retired. Most of my life I had

Robert Baillie

sailed the Arctic frozen wastes and I would certainly miss the comradeship of the brave men I had sailed with and also the friends I had worked with while Klondiking.

On Wednesday, August 2 I had a telephone call asking me to go and see our Klondiking operational manager at the Livingston Road headquarters. He wanted to discuss my retirement and whether I would go back to Ullapool for another season.

When I left his office, I had agreed to go back for another season in the company of our 'overseer of accommodation' in Ullapool, my wife Rita. We had now been together on this project for a few years. And on Tuesday, September 5, I received another call, this time from Captain David Hinchcliffe from Lerwick, to arrange the details of my return to Ullapool.

On Friday, September 8 I celebrated another birthday. I was 65 years old and had been working for 51 years. I could have been enjoying my retirement. But on Saturday, September 16 at 09.30 I left Hessle for Ullapool to start my final season Klondiking...

CHAPTER 20
TIME TO RETIRE?

In September 1989 I celebrated my 65th birthday and as far as the state was concerned I was officially retired. But even after 51 years of working, I planned to do one more season Klondiking in Ullapool.

On Sunday, September 17 Rita and I arrived at Myrtle Cottage for the last time and the following day I was back on the pier base. But I was also informed that Myrtle Cottage was going to be my headquarters again. A telephone and communication sets were installed in the spare room and I carried out all my night work from my cottage. I did not need to leave it at all. It was a last bit of luxury in my closing months of duty.

The pair trawlers 'Quiet Waters' and 'Steadfast Hope' arrived with their first catches of herring, closely followed by Jasper Sea and on Sunday, September 24 my old friend Angus in Orcadius Viking.

By September 26 a lot of boats had caught their herring quota with Vic in Omega being one of the last to arrive back in port. There was then a bit of a lull in Ullapool but in Lerwick the fishing was yet to start. They had been given a mackerel quota of 35,000 tonnes and most of the Eastern Block ships had returned for the start of the season and were ready to take this quota on board.

By Tuesday, October 3 there was plenty of herring coming in but we also had a lot of Klondikers going to Lerwick for mackerel. We were left with only two Russians, the big factory ship Vasilisen and the Tamula.

Quo Vadis arrived with 120 ton of herring but my old pals Quiet Waters and Steadfast Hope had now gone home. And by Friday, October 27 there were no vessels fishing at all at Ullapool.

Robert Baillie

The next day, a full storm was blowing and the Ullapool to Stornoway ferry was storm bound in Ullapool and couldn't sail. In fact no boats were sailing from Ullapool so there was only mackerel fishing at Lerwick until the quota had been taken. I was informed that would happen around Saturday, November 4. So we waited for Lerwick to finish and the return of the Klondikers to Ullapool.

On Sunday, November 5 Lerwick finished but there was a lot of fish still to land. We also had a number of Dutch and Irish fishing vessels arriving in Ullapool.

The following day, the Klondikers arrived back in Ullapool and anchored in Annat Bay ready to take the mackerel when it arrived. And by Tuesday, November 7 there was plenty of mackerel coming in from the north, so we prepared to take it.

I left the cottage to do the nightshift in P & J Johnstone's offices on the pier. And as we had the Klondikers arriving in company with the Scots Pursers loaded with mackerel, as soon as the Russians had anchored, we began discharging the boats. So began another season. Ullapool was full and buzzing again as I started Klondiking for the last time.

The Russian factory ships we had operating for us included Victor Kingisepp, Rybatskyaslava, and Dzintarura. The Dutch ships included Alida, Ariadne, Gertrude and Margarita and the Irish boats included Annya, Father McGee, Western Viking, Sheanne and Paula. We were also informed the ETAs of Bulgarians, Germans and the pursers, Orcadius Viking, Star Crest, Quo Vadis, Christina S. and Sedulous.

We had Coronella in port requiring a diver and the big Russian factory ship Professor Baranofhad arrived. It was then back to full nightshift work. Get the fishing boats discharged quickly, order their fuel and stores when they had finished and order buses if the crews were going home. Then make sure the Russians were anchored in the proper position. The order of the day was move the boats quickly and get them discharged, then back to sea to catch some more fish and make sure the Russian factory ships were always working. That meant no hold-ups, no mistakes, be on your toes all the time, make your decisions quickly and always stay alert.

The only snag was that the mackerel was still away to the north, a great distance from Ullapool that resulted in long steams for the catching vessels. It also meant using more fuel so the purser had to get a big catch for it to be viable. And as we needed to constantly take catches to keep the big Russian factory ships working, we hoped that the mackerel would move south.

The other news that we did not want to hear was that the weather in the north was bad. The Scottish fish catchers were all anchored in Yell Sound, so there was no fishing to the north and we were left with only a few herring boats fishing closer to base.

On Monday, November 20 our information was that the fish was 30 hours steam from Ullapool up at Balta in the Shetlands. The only bright news was that the weather had improved and there was a small amount of mackerel arriving. The latest information was that some fish had been caught north of Rona but the mackerel was small so fishing was still concentrated around the Shetlands.

Things remained slack in Ullapool until around November 29 when the mackerel started to arrive and by the following day a lot of fish had arrived.

On Friday, December 1 Ullapool was full again and it was full steam ahead to get the fish landed. We worked continuously directing this huge influx of fish to the appropriate factory vessels and by Tuesday 5, we had cleared it. After that, there was only the odd ship arriving with fish.

On Friday, December 8, the Fishing Authorities announced that all fishing was to cease at midnight. Gunboats were out to enforce this rule so all we could do was wait until midnight and see which boats arrived with their catches at Ullapool. Orcadius Viking arrived with 750 tonnes of fish on board along with Coronella, Star Crest and Sedulous. It was then work away until all these boats were discharged.

On Wednesday 13, all herring fishing stopped and by Friday, December 15 all fishing had ceased. The last vessel to land its catch was the Omega on Sunday, December 17 and there was no more fishing until January 1990. Most of our staff left Ullapool but as usual Rita and I remained in our cottage and spent the last Christmas and New Year of our working lives there.

By Thursday, December 21, the Klondiking staff had also gone home and the only two ships left with me were the Russian factory ship Rybatskayslava and the Russian Klondiker 'Bizon'. These two would be available when the Irish fishing vessels arrived on December 29.

It was now time for Rita and I to get our Christmas tree, trimmings, turkey and spirits for our last festive season in Ullapool. We then decorated the cottage and prepared to welcome all of our friends for a dram or two.

On December 23, it was also our wedding anniversary. It was 39 years since coming off the trawler Kingston Sardius for dry-docking and getting married during my short stay in dock. One week later I sailed to Bear Island and luckily made our first £10,000 voyage. The time had flown by so quickly…

Everything was now ready for the Christmas

break. We had even sent out some fir trees to the 'Rybatskayslava' and 'Bizon'. But then suddenly on our wedding anniversary the wind increased to storm force and remained with us until Christmas Day. It then abated for a few hours before increasing again to force nine. That meant that nobody could get out until Boxing Day when the winds decreased and resulted in a late visit to our friends' houses.

On Sunday, December 31 the first Irish boat, 'The Antarctic' arrived and after the usual inspection by the fishery officers, went straight to the Rybatskayslava, where he commenced to discharge his catch of mackerel. We now had information that plenty of mackerel was coming to Ullapool from Ireland and the Shetland Isles.

On January 5, the Spez Magna, Quo Vadis, Sedulous, Coronella, Christina S, Orcadius Viking, all arrived loaded with mackerel. And waiting for them and ready to take this huge amount of fish were the Russian ships including Servelod, Karpaty and Rudolph Sergi, that had just returned from the Russian ports. For over four days we landed this fish with all boats working to full capacity including our old friend the Dutch factory vessel 'Prince Bernhard' anchored off the pier in Loch Broom.

So once again Ullapool was full with boats at the Pier waiting their turn to discharge. Factory vessels calling us to report that they had taken enough. Others declaring what time they would be starting again, probably after a few hours of 'waiting time'. Boats that had discharged, now requiring fuel and stores. Boats going home for the weekend, anchoring inside and their crews requiring bus transport. Boats wanting repairs, engineers, shipwrights, radio and radar technicians - and even divers to check problems with damaged propellers.

Robert Baillie

This was Klondiking! Day and night it never stopped...

On January 9 we were hit by more stormy weather. It continued until January 21 and stopped all fishing except for a few herring boats fishing close to Ullapool. Most of the others anchored until the storm abated or simply went home.

On January 23 the winds decreased and our first boat in was the Irish, Atlanteen that proceeded to Victor Kingisepp to discharge.

The reports were now of good mackerel fishing and on Saturday, January 27 the pursers Coronella, Radiant Way, Quo Vadis, Spez Magna, Christina S., Sedulous, Omega, Orcadius Viking and Jasper Sea arrived. They were a very welcome sight after all the stormy weather. We worked flat out to discharge this huge tonnage of mackerel but alas on January 31 things were once again interrupted by stormy weather. In fact by Saturday, February 3 due to the terrible weather, all fishing boat crews had gone home.

On February 5 at 03.00 hours, all our electric went off. There was no panic of course, we reverted to the candles and paraffin heaters, and the sandwiches and flasks of tea from our good neighbour Alice McGregor. At 10:00 hours the electric came on again but I wondered for how long?

On Tuesday, February 6, the storm had decreased and all the fishing vessels were back on the fishing grounds. The reports from the grounds were good, so thankfully we could again expect quite a bit of mackerel arriving at Ullapool. Meanwhile our herring boat Steadfast Hope had arrived with herring and our pursers had reported in by radio that they were on their way with some big catches.

By the Friday, Ullapool was literally full of

mackerel again. This lasted us a few days and thank goodness this fish had arrived. Strong to gale force westerly winds were forecast and as a result the smaller Russian ships were anchored inside Ullapool. This suited the purser skippers, as they would be in calmer waters to land their catches.

This operation would be my last, as I was due to retire on February 15. I was still doing constant nightshifts, 22.00 to 08:00 hours, seven days a week from my base in Myrtle Cottage. Discharging this lot wasn't so bad as the Russians were 'empty', due to the fact that no fish had been arriving because of the stormy weather. So there was no waiting time and they could start the usual procedure immediately. The pursers booked into the fishery office. The fishery officers went out to them to inspect their catch. Then we directed the fishing boat to a Russian ship for discharge. The purser's tanks were opened and the operation commenced. This continued until all the fishing boats were alongside their designated Russian factory ship and discharging. I had been doing this for ten years and had never had a dull moment.

On Sunday, February 11 the winds had again reached storm force so there was no more fish arriving at Ullapool. I had only five days left before my retirement. So while Ullapool was quiet due to the storms, I thought I would do a round of all my old friends before I departed for good. I started of course with Harry McRae, the boatman who brought me ashore off my old ship Cordella on my first day in Ullapool and who now owned and operated a successful boat company supplying the Klondiking fleet.

Next was Donnie McLeod the harbourmaster and John McLeod who had ran the small grocery shop when I first arrived but now was an invaluable supplier to the entire Klondiking operation.

Robert Baillie

Then, all my friends on the pier, my great friend Mattison at the Argyle Hotel, Billy McRae - one of the top inshore shellfishers, American Mike - the radio and radar technician, Donald MacDonald - the manager of Caley Fisheries and all my close friends at P & J Johnstone Fishing, whom I had worked with during my stay in Ullapool. The list went on and on.

After six years with me in this unique operation, Rita also had to see her friends before leaving. They of course included Alice McGregor, our next door neighbour who had served us well during our electricity cuts and who we both always remembered as a truly great friend and a marvellous woman. Marilyn, who owned the Loch View Guesthouse near our cottage where we were both invited many times for dinner. And our special friends, George and Rosanna Ross who owned Myrtle Cottage and always made our seasonal stay in Ullapool a comfortable one. We would certainly miss this beautiful, highland fishing port and the warm welcome of its people when we arrived each season.

I woke up on Friday, February 16, 1990 knowing it was the last day of my working life. It was my retirement day. My final day in 'the fishing world'. And after 43 years' service to the fishing industry, 33 years' sailing and 10 years with the Klondike fleet, it was now time to pack up my gear for the last time. Rita and I had been away from home for five months.

The weather in Ullapool was still very stormy so there was no fishing. Most of the boats were moored alongside the pier or anchored in the bay.

During my last morning, I had a visit from our management team led by Captain Harry Harrison and Captain Tony Atkinson. They informed me that at 20:00 hours they would pick up Rita and I and take us to the Harbour Lights Hotel for a retirement drink before we left for the final time.

WAITING FOR THE TIDE

That evening at exactly 8pm a car arrived and we were both driven to the Harbour Lights. When we entered the small cocktail bar there was a few of our friends there to meet us. We enjoyed a quiet drink but then received our first surprise.

The owners of the hotel, our great friends Marlene and Danny, came through and Danny said, 'Right Bob and Rita, come through here with me.'

We followed him through to the adjoining room, where there was a bigger surprise, with around sixty people waiting for us. They seemed to include everyone that we had ever dealt with, from Russian, Dutch and Bulgarian captains to reps from the fishing companies. The guests were lined up down each side of the room and in the centre was a table for Rita and me, with the most magnificent galleon on it, made by a Russian which had taken him nearly two years to make. At the end of the room was a huge buffet.

We took our seats, then after a few speeches from various guests we received a presentation of retirement cards and faxes from Marr executives from as far away as Bermuda and Canada. The last card that we received was presented by my great friend off the pursers, Vic Buscini. The card had about fifteen skippers' names on it and entitled Rita and I to a holiday anywhere in the world, paid for by the named skippers. It was certainly a fantastic and very memorable present. But as Rita didn't like flying we eventually settled on another visit to our favourite place - Scotland.

After a few drinks it was buffet time and what an excellent spread it was. Then, following the buffet, we were taken through to another room for the next surprise, a disco with some splendid music that went on until 3am.

It was a great night and near the end I got the call for a speech. So there I was in my usual stance with a

Robert Baillie

Department of Transport
Marine Office
Posterngate
Kingston Upon Hull HU1 2LN

Telephone 0482 223066 (3 Lines)
Telex 52478 Answer back code 52478 DTHULL G   592478

Fax : 219912

F A O: A L Marr
North Atlantic Fishing Company Limited
10 St Andrew's Dock
HULL
North Humberside
HU3 6PN.

Please Reply to THE CHIEF SUP

Your reference   -

Our reference   GMD / PAL

Date   25 August 1988

Dear Sirs

M. V. " WESTELLA " O N 712675

Thank you for your letters of 24 August.

We can confirm that Mr Baillie's qualifications will meet the Department's requirements for a General Certificate Radiotelephone Operator to be aboard when the vessel is engaged in Klondyking activities.

Your application for exemption from the fitting of a direction finder and homing device, has been forwarded to the Department's Navigation and Communications Branch in London, with a favourable recommendation.

We will let you know the outcome as soon as possible.

Yours faithfully

G M DOLAN
Senior Radio Surveyor

encl, PMG Certificate + other documents belonging to Mr R Baillie.

microphone. I gave my speech then ended it with my usual call that I'd given over the last 10 years, 'This is Marr Base.' But this time my call had a different ending.

'This is Marr Base, over and out and thanks to you all.'

Before leaving there were another two surprises. While working at the base on the pier I often mentioned that I would get a greenhouse on my retirement. And to my delight a present from my friend Derrick Bond at P and J was an envelope containing £280 to purchase a greenhouse. But as well as that, the galleon on the table was also another present to me. I couldn't believe it. And last of all, a bottle of 10-year-old whiskey. What a retirement!

The next morning I received a final present from George and Rosanna Ross, a beautiful brass yacht on a block of fine stone. I could not have wished for a better send-off...

Saturday, February 17 finally arrived.

Well, this was it, the day when I retired. When all my fishing adventures were over. We now had to pack up for the very last time. Ten years of Klondiking had come to an end.

I stepped out of Myrtle Cottage and looked over Loch Broom towards Annat Bay and thought about the huge operation we had come through.

The Scots' pursers and the trawlers arriving full of mackerel. The bustle of discharging to the Russians, Bulgarians, Poles, East Germans and Romanians. The storms. The long days and nights. Supplying all those ships from our base ashore.

Was I glad that I was leaving?

I wasn't sure that I was. After all, this was my life. The sea, the smell of the ships, the endless day and night activities.

Robert Baillie

I went back into Myrtle Cottage, sat down and pondered about the past few years. Then, after Rita and I had packed, I wandered down to the Argyle Hotel and the pier to say my final farewells to all my friends and have a last look round.

A couple of hours later, back at Myrtle Cottage we received a storm warning. It proved to be the final irony. The approaching bad weather made it impossible for us to leave and we did not get away until three days later. But then, as I finally drove away from Ullapool for the very last time, I gazed back through the car's mirror at the life I was leaving behind.

The scene looked perfect.

Memories of Russian convoys on HMS Trumpeter, spying on the Russian Navy and freezing on countless trawlers in the Arctic wastes ran through my mind.

The storm had now abated and the loch, framed by a spectacular, golden sunset was calm again. And away in the distance, the dark silhouette of the last remaining Russian ship floated almost motionless on the shimmering water.

It seemed that some things never changed...

EPILOGUE

The journey south was good. On Tuesday night we stopped at our favourite hotel in Lauderdale before completing our journey on Wednesday and arriving back in Hessle at around 5pm.

I now had 'a retired shoreman's life' to look forward to.

I feared that it might prove to be a bit monotonous when compared to the life I'd lived. But I had my family to take care of and my allotment to work on and this took up the majority of my time. And as the 1990s rolled on, a wonderful event occurred. My granddaughter Lisa had a baby boy, our first great-grandson, Liam. I named him 'The Laird of Scotland'.

Lisa, her partner Chris and 'The Laird' moved into their own house about 200 yards from ours. This was Rita's and my greatest reward.

As The Laird grew older he used to sleep at our house every Saturday night. It was then that he asked me if I could tell him one of my sea yarns. This I did.

Here was the great idea I had of why not write him a book of all the sea yarns, and as I kept a diary every day of my life this was not a problem.

So as I conclude my story, I dedicate it to Liam and to all the brave fishermen I sailed with and especially to those whom I saw die whilst fishing in the horrendous conditions of the Arctic seas.

Me and my grandson Liam, 'The Laird'